Remembering Monty Hall:

# Let’s Make a Deal

Written by Ken Rotcop

and Kimberly Kaplan

“Mensch: an upright man or woman; a gentleman; a decent human being (from Yiddish מענטש mentsh ‘person’ and German Mensch: human being); the generic term for a virtuous man or person; one with honesty, integrity, loyalty, firmness of purpose: a fundamental sense of decency and respect for other people.”

~ Leo Rosten “The Joys of Yiddish”

Monty Hall was a mensch.

Published in the USA by:
BearManor Media
P O Box 71426
Albany, Georgia 31708
www.bearmanormedia.com

Printed in the United States of America
ISBN 978-1-62933-422-6 (Paperback)
978-1-62933-423-3 (Hardcover)

Book and cover design by Darlene Swanson • www.van-garde.com

# Acknowledgments

WHEN IT COMES TO writing a biography it takes the collaboration of a lot of people to make it happen. So it was with this manuscript.

Let me start with Monty Hall's children: Richard Hall, Sharon Hall, and Joanna Gleason. Besides sharing family photos and anecdotes, they played *Your First Impression* with us, sharing insights into Monty that are fun and oh so human. Their enthusiasm for the project got the ball rolling, for which I thank them.

And thanks to Carol Merrill, who was with Monty on *Let's Make a Deal* for fourteen years, and Hank Koval, working behind the scenes for Monty and was with him even longer.

And thanks to Brian Huber at the University of Manitoba, who shared articles and photos from his Monty Hall collection with us. And then there was Monty's first cousin, Dr. Jack Rusen, who told us stories about Monty that we had never heard before.

And thanks to Monty's brother, Bob, who said they grew up so poor they always wore Army surplus clothes. He remembers how embarrassed Monty was to wear Canadian Army fatigue shirts that were too big and pants that were too long. But somehow he and Bob survived, didn't they?

And yet another big thank you to Dan Klein, a man of so many talents he should be writing a book about himself. He has always been there for me whether it's fixing a door knob or taping an audio of one of my books or creating the covers of my last three books. He is more than a friend, he is a brother.

And then, of course, there is Rachel Wolf, my personal assistant who runs my business life and keeps my career from careening off the tracks into oblivion. I thank her every day, especially when she sits in front of the computer manipulating that machine to make sense and bring order to my confusion.

And a great big thank you to The Bulldog. She doesn't know that's what I call her, but leaving no stone unturned, that's the way Kimberly Kaplan handled the job of finding people for this book, tracking them down, keeping after them once she found them, prodding and nudging to get them to share their stories, anecdotes, and photos, then getting those stories and pictures to me to include in this tome. And doing much of it while on vacation in Hawaii! Way to go, Bulldog!

And finally, to my wife, Connie, whose life I share when I'm not closeted in my office writing, or teaching at the local college, or off lecturing somewhere, or preparing my play for production, or running a workshop, or ensconced in front of the TV watching a ballgame. Thank you, Connie, for always being there for me and putting up with my nonsense.

# Contents

Monty with mother Rose (cir.1928).]

# Introduction

I WAS IN ACAPULCO on my honeymoon when the phone rang in our suite. I couldn't imagine who would be calling me in Mexico.

"Ken, it's Wes." Wes Kenny was the best man at our wedding. "What are you doing?"

"What do you mean 'What am I doing?!' I'm on my honeymoon!"

"Can you come back to LA? Can you be here by Monday?"

"Maybe we have a bad connection. I said I'm on my honeymoon."

Wes heard me alright. He just ignored me. "The writer on the show I'm directing decided to take a three-week sabbatical and we need a writer. I thought you might—"

"Wes, you're doing a game show. You're telling me game shows have writers?"

"I'll tell you all about it when you get here."

I raised my voice. "I'm on my honeymoon! Remember? You were my best man!"

"You said you always wanted to come to Hollywood to write. Here's your chance. Come to the NBC building Monday. Ask for me."

He hung up.

My new bride was down by the pool. If I hadn't come up to get the sunscreen I would have missed the call.

I called Jerry Mandell in New York. Jerry and I were partners in Concepts, Inc., an entertainment advertising agency at 535 5th Avenue.

"Jerry, it's Ken."

"How's the honeymoon?"

"Listen, Jerry, I've got a chance to go to LA for three weeks to write a game show."

"They have writers on game shows?"

"Of course they have writers on game shows! Look, can you hold the fort down for another three weeks?"

"Is Susan disappointed?"

I sighed. "I haven't told her yet."

"All her life she wanted to live in New York and now you're depriving her—"

I raised my voice. "Three weeks! Three weeks!"

Jerry loved to give me a hard time. "Some honeymoon," he said.

"I know."

We arrived at LAX and I went straight to the NBC studios in Burbank.

Wes greeted me.

"How was the honeymoon?"

"All three days? Outside of the fact the wife isn't talking to me it was fine."

Wes clued me in. The game was called *Your First Impression* and it featured a panel such as Dennis James, Rose Marie, and George

Kirko trying to guess the identity of a hidden celebrity in a soundproof booth behind them.

The panel would read the beginning of a statement and the hidden celebrity would fill in the rest of the sentence.

For instance: "I really get upset when…" and the celebrity would finish with the first thing that came to their mind.

Or: "If you want to see me blush, remind me of the time I…"

Or one more. "You're my kind of gal if…"

And based on their responses the panel would guess who the celebrity was.

And my job? Write these half-sentences and come up with witty introductions of the celebrities and the panel for Bill Leyden, the host.

But the best part of the job was preparing the guest celebrities.

I would go to their homes and play the game with them by giving them a different set of half-statements, not the ones they would get on the show.

So one day I'd be having lunch with Stella Stevens, or sitting in Bob Hope's house, or driving around Beverly Hills with Mort Sahl, or sipping hot tea with Robert Taylor or Ida Lapino and Howard Duff, or meeting Shirley Jones in a restaurant, or playing the game with Don Rickles. But I'm getting ahead of myself. That first day, Wes took me around and I met the staff.

"I want you to meet our producer."

He took me into the biggest office.

"Monte, this is the writer I told you about."

"Ken, say hello to Monty Hall."

And suddenly I had my first job in Hollywood. Me, who had never watched a game show on television, was now a game show writer!

In those three weeks I spent a lot of time around Monty. In groups. By ourselves. In his office. At the studio. In the green room. On the set.

He loved to tell stories. Stories about growing up and getting started in Canada. Stories that I promise to share with you.

And I guess I did a decent job. I guess I wrote decent half-sentences, because Monty fired the writer who took the sabbatical and asked me to stay on.

I didn't go back to New York for many years, much to the disappointment of my bride. I sold my half of my ad agency to my partner, Jerry.

I learned many things working for Monty. One thing was, never go on a sabbatical when you're working on a TV show. Your job may not be there when you come back.

My first Hollywood lesson. And my first Hollywood job.

Thanks, Monty!

# The Scandal

Let's go back to 1958.

The hottest game show on television was *Twenty-One*. Two contestants competed against each other by answering questions on an endless number of subjects. Both contestants were in separate, isolated, soundproof booths and both wore headphones. The idea was that neither could hear the other's answers, nor did they know which one was winning. The tougher the question, the more points (1 to 10) awarded for a correct answer. First to twenty-one won.

The show was produced by Jack Barry and Dan Enright and Barry was the host. The initial show was a bomb! The contestants were awful—maybe stupid's a better word—and the show was a dismal failure. Geratol, the sponsor of the show, was furious and threatened to pull the game off the air immediately. So Barry and Enright sat in Enright's office and knew they had to come up with a quick fix.

And "fix" was the key word.

"What if we give the contestants the answers before the show?"

"Can we do that?"

"We gotta do something."

"Both contestants?"

"Maybe just one. And maybe he wins week after week so we build an audience and we build suspense. Like, is there anyone who can knock him off?!"

"Should we tell Al? Should he know?"

Al was Albert Freedman, who was actually the producer of the show.

"Yeah, Al should know."

"And the director?"

"No, he doesn't have to know."

"We can get in trouble, you know."

"We gotta make sure the contestants we pick get paid off good and know to keep their mouths shut."

"And what happens," asked Jack Barry, "when I leave the show? Remember I'm taking three weeks for my nightclub tour."

"First of all, we'll probably be off the air by then."

"And if we're not? What do we tell my replacement?"

"Nothing. He needs to know nothing. He should look astonished when the same contestant wins week after week."

"Sounds good."

"Who did we get? Tom Kennedy?"

"Not available. Monty Hall."

"Any good?"

"Yeah, he does a lot of summer replacement hosting. He's alright."

So Monty got his first big break. By the time he hosted the show, just as predicted, it had shot to number one in America and Monty was seen by millions of people.

And Jack Barry, who started as a singer, fell in love with playing nightclubs. He decided not to come back to *Twenty-One* and Monty was hired full-time.

Monty made big money…for a month. It was at that time that New York newspapers broke the story of the fix.

One disgruntled contestant went to the district attorney's office and blew the lid off the quiz show.

He charged that contestants were given the answers in advance, and said he was also bribed to purposely lose to a more popular contestant but was promised a job with Barry-Enright organization if he would give a wrong answer to a question and let the other guy win.

So he lost on purpose. But they never offered him a job.

He was angry. Angry and disappointed. So he went to the D.A.

When the story broke, guess who else was angry and disappointed? Monty couldn't believe these shenanigans were going on right under his nose and he never had a clue. The advertising agency representing Geratol, the sponsor, asked Monty to come to the agency for a meeting.

"We've been meeting nonstop for two days now. The people at Geratol want Jack Barry back."

"Why?"

"They think it looks bad the boss of the show is off running around the country singing in clubs and lounges while the government is investigating his show. Sorry, Monty."

So Monty was fired.

And the scandal spread. Other former contestants on other big money giveaway shows came forth. They too had been swindled.

Barry and Enright, having pleaded guilty to swindling the public, saw their show cancelled, and the two fled Los Angeles, Enright to Cancun and Barry eventually to Florida. Albert Freedman moved to Mexico.

It was ten years before Barry and Enright came back to Los Angeles to renew their partnership.

*Twenty-One* wasn't the only show cancelled. *Dotto*, cancelled. *$64,000 Challenge* and *$64,000 Question*, cancelled. And another Barry-Enright show, *Tic-Tac-Dough*, also cancelled.

All went down the second half of 1958.

The country that loved quiz shows in those early years of television now turned against them and their ratings plummeted before the networks yanked them off.

There was a group of us having bagels and coffee in the First Impression office when the conversation turned to the game show scandals of 1958. When Monty spoke up I, frankly, was surprised by his take.

"I think people like Barry and Enright were treated much too harshly. I mean, I know what they did was a wrong. I know they were guilty. But who was hurt by those shows? Weren't people entertained? Isn't that what television is for? Was it any more fake than wrestling or roller derby or any of these magic shows? Yes, I'd put the Barrys and the Enrights on probation, but they were blacklisted for about ten years. Guilty of trying to entertain their audience. Too harsh."

The death of the quiz game show meant the networks were looking for something different.

No more questions and answers. No more big money to the winners.

What was needed was a different type of game show. Something that you didn't have to be super smart to play. Something the common man could identify with. Games that didn't have right or wrong answers.

And hosts that had to be glib, fast on their feet. Not just stand at a podium and read questions off a card.

No one was better to host this kind of show than Monty. If only he could create one!

Monty (cir. 1945)

# The Hockey Games

The year was 1931.

"Welcome, ladies and gentlemen, to the brand new Maple Leaf Gardens for tonight's game between the Toronto Blue Jays and the Montreal Maroons. The game is about to begin and here's your play-by-play announcer, the voice of the Toronto Maple Leafs, Monte Halparin."

"Thanks, Sam. The game is about to begin. The puck is dropped and Joe Prime of the Leafs swings it over to Busher Jackson, who carries into Montreal territory. There's a quick pass to Charlie Conacher who shoots and SCORES! Maple Leafs one, Maroons nothing!"

It's dark, freezing cold, and lightly snowing as a ten-year-old boy peddles his bike through the streets of Winnipeg, Manitoba, Canada. He's delivering kosher meats, for his father is the neighborhood butcher and he's his father's delivery boy.

To pass the time, to not think about the lashing wind, the falling snow, or the gloomy streets, Monte Halparin talks to himself. Or better yet, announces and does the radio play-by-play of a hockey game that he makes up in his head. It makes the times of delivery go faster, he forgets the elements and his surroundings, imagining he's at the Maple Leaf Gardens, and best of all, the games that Monte "broadcasts," the Maple Leafs always win!

It's now 1959.

High above the ice rink at Madison Square Garden in New York City, two men sit in front of their mics. A radio engineer points to one of the men. He's on.

"Welcome, ladies and gentlemen, to Madison Square Garden, where tonight our New York Rangers take on the Boston Bruins."

It's Monty doing the color on New York radio of Ranger hockey games. The ten-year-old boy who made up hockey broadcasts was now doing it for real!

How'd Monty get the job?

Well, besides hosting *Twenty-One*, Monty signed a contract with Channel Five in New York to do a terribly boring show called *Bingo at Home*, where Monty's job was a to pull ping pong balls with numbers on them out of a machine, and if you could match the numbers with your telephone number, you won. It was the lowest rated show in its time slot and the show died.

Monty hated the job, knew the show was boring, but, hey, he needed the job and needed the money.

But then he got *Twenty-One* till that was cancelled, so he had a few bucks in his pocket.

Plus, he was getting a check from a syndicated show he had running in Canada called *Who Am I?*

When Bingo was dropped Monty sold Channel Five on an interview show that he would host. His guests would be celebrities and politicians, but that show failed also.

But Monty still had more time on his contract with Channel Five. So to fulfill his obligation they sent Monty off to Sunnyside Gardens in Queens every week to do the play-by-play, blow-by-blow, body slam-by-body slam of the professional wrestling matches!

As Monty said, "It was a job."

Although the matches were fake, the wrestlers were outlandish, the fans weird. Monty played it straight, reporting every match like it was the seventh game of the World Series.

One day he gets a call from Les Keiter of WINS Radio.

"Monty, I saw you on those wrestling matches."

"Well, it's not really—"

"No, no. You're good. Very good."

"Thank you."

"There's a job open as color man for the New York Rangers."

Monty couldn't believe what he was hearing. Was he about to make an offer?

Keiter continued, "I know you're a Canuck, so I assume you know something about hockey. Did you ever broadcast hockey games?"

Monty got the job.

Monty did the color and Jim Gordon did the play-by-play. They worked together for two years, Monty just doing the home games. It brought him back to those gloomy, bitter cold, snowy evenings in Winnipeg when Monty, riding his bike, delivered the packages of meat from his father's butcher shop, announcing Maple Leaf hockey games to himself.

As Monty once told me, "I got paid, I think it was, $50 a game. But, honestly, as broke as I was, I would have done the games for free."

# Max Freed

I GUESS OF ALL the stories Monty told, the one that made the greatest impression on me was the story he told us about a man named Max Freed.

Monty was 17, graduating from high school and wanting to go to the University of Manitoba to study medicine. Only one thing was stopping him. He had no money. No money for tuition, for clothes, for textbooks, or for transportation.

His mother worked in the butcher shop answering the phone, taking orders. When a customer would call, Rose, Monty's mother, would ask them if they would like to contribute money to send her son, Monty, to college. All donations, she told them, would be applicable against future orders.

Three customers came through, each with a $50 contribution. The $150 was just enough to cover tuition.

Other money came from nickels and dimes that Rose had saved over the years, as well as some money his father, Maurice, had put aside. Somehow the family scraped enough to send Monty to college.

His clothes were all hand-me-downs from his cousins and uncles, his textbooks secondhand.

But when college began, off Monty went every morning at the crack of dawn, taking the streetcar to the university. And he did well. Got good grades, home in time for supper, studying, and off to bed.

On weekends he worked in his dad's butcher shop. In the summer he worked full-time for his dad. His salary? Nothing. There was no salary.

So when it came time to return to school for his sophomore year Monty had to drop out. The family simply did not have enough money to send him.

Monty had to get a full-time job that paid him a salary.

Close to his house was a wholesale garment manufacturing plant that had a *Help Wanted* sign posted in their window.

Monty got the job. Salary? Nine dollars a week. Since he could walk to work, live at home, and skimp on lunches, Monty figured to save five or six dollars a week.

Monty swept the floors, crated clothing, carried boxes from the factory to the shipping dock and from the shipping dock to the factory, folded merchandise, unfolded merchandise, made deliveries, and washed the shelves and counters. But it was a job. And he was getting paid.

One afternoon while Monty was on his hands and knees scrubbing the grime off the front steps he noticed a young man in front of the wholesale house directly across the street watching him.

Monty knew all about him. Actually, everybody in Winnipeg knew all about him. He was handsome, a bachelor, and at 29 was very wealthy. If Manitoba had a Great Gatsby, it was this guy. Seen at all the "in" parties, dining at all the top restaurants, always escorting the prettiest, most influential young women about town, hanging out at the race track. He was, without doubt, the most hated, envied, intensely despised man in town.

His father had made a fortune and turned everything over to his son when the boy was twenty one. The boy wanted for nothing and his father gave him the world.

The "kid" worked hard and ran a very successful business. But the busy-bodies and rumor mongers and envious men of Winnipeg couldn't care less.

"He's wasting his ol' man's money."

"If he hadn't been spoon-fed he'd probably be out digging ditches."

"It's disgusting how he throws his father's money around."

"He'll be broke by the time he's forty, you mark my words!"

And so it went.

Max had one passion. Even greater than women, liquor, and good parties, Max loved horses. Thoroughbred horses. Racing horses. When he could, he bought Maxwell King Stables and bred and raced hundreds of winners all across Canada.

One evening as the Halperin family sat down for dinner Monty's father said to Monty, "Guess who I ran into today?"

"I don't know. Who?"

"Max Freed."

"Who?"

"Max Freed, the young man who has the wholesale house right across from yours."

"Oh, yeah. I've seen him in front of his place." And then, with a cockney accent, "A real dandy, that one."

Monty's father ignored the wisecrack. "He wants to meet you."

"Me?"

"He said he noticed what a hard worker you were. Wanted to know why you were working at such a piss-poor place."

"Did he actually say 'piss-poor'?"

"Well, something like that. Anyway, he asked why you weren't going to college."

"And," Monty cut in, "you said…?"

"I told him the truth. We didn't have the money to send you. He asked what kind of grades you got in school and I told him you were an A student. He seemed to like that. Anyway, he wants you to come see him tomorrow."

Instead of lunch the next day Monty walked across the street and met the infamous Max Freed.

"Your father said your family has no money."

"We get by."

"For a family with no money, what was he doing playing poker?"

"Is that were you met him? At a men's club?"

"It is."

"It's one of his few joys. And he knows his limits."

What else could Monty say? I really never knew if Monty knew his dad played poker or not.

Max changed the subject. "You want to go back to college?"

"I wish I could."

"What would you study?"

"Medicine."

"You want to be a doctor?"

"Yes."

Max sighed. "You know about the quota, I assume."

"If I get straight A's…"

Max studied Monty. He knew he was about to say something to Monty that would change Monty's whole life.

"I will pay whatever it is for you to go back to college."

Was Monty stunned?! What do you think?

After making sure he heard Max correctly, Monty stammered, "I… I don't understand."

"You will go to the University of Manitoba for as long as it takes you to get your degree. Take a full schedule of classes, sign up for any extracurricular activities that you feel will be beneficial, and start with the new semester."

"What's the hook?" asked Monty suspiciously.

"I'll get to that at another time. But for now give me a breakdown in a couple of days of what it will cost for tuition and books and for clothes, and include weekly expenses: food, a haircut, anything you can think of. When you have figured it out come back and I will give you the money."

Monty thought the whole thing was too easy. *Maybe*, he thought to himself, *Max Freed is a quack. Nuts!*

A couple of days later Monty brought Max the list.

"You didn't put anything down for new clothes."

"I don't need new clothes," Monty protested.

"Of course you do! Let's double the expense money and get you a couple of suits."

Now it was Monty's turn. "Why, Max, are you doing this? You hardly know me. I'm sure you took pity on me when you'd see me scraping and washing the front steps. Hell, I took pity on myself! But…why?"

"I know the way the people in Winnipeg talk about me. Poor little rich kid never earned a dollar in his life. Spends all his dad's hard earned money living the easy life. And on and on. In truth, I've more than doubled our business' earnings, expanded our markets, tripled our inventory, but nobody cares about that side of me.

It's true I've had everything in life given to me, so now I'd like to help others less fortunate.

"And, incidentally, you're not the first. There were two other students who took up my offer but they both dropped out of college, took my money and ran.

"Monty, don't disappoint me. Promise me you'll stay with it until you become a doctor or at least a graduate."

Monty measured his words carefully. "You said there were 'conditions' that I must perform."

"Ah, yes. First, you must report to me on the first of every month and show me your grades. Drop below a B and our deal will come to an end."

"And second?"

"Second is you must eventually pay me back every single dollar. And there's more. Monty, you must promise to help others some day as I am helping you. When you become a doctor you must remember poor people get sick too, not just the rich. And finally, you must never tell anyone, except your parents, about our arrangement."

Was he nuts? Or just a man grateful for his good fortune and felt obligated—or maybe guilt-ridden—to pull some poor wretch up from the ashes… In this case, Monty Halperin.

Monty said the man never made a move on him, which, of course, also came to his mind.

The fact that he didn't want anyone to know of his good deed always intrigued Monty. Why not let the "good folks" of Winnipeg know about this side of Max Freed? Why not, indeed?

So Monty got to live the life of a college student. He even knew the luxury of having a few dollars in his wallet. And Monty continued to help his dad out in the butcher shop on Saturdays and even worked one day a week at Max's place.

Did Monty fulfill his promise? Well, yes and no.

Because of the quota system he never went to medical school. His life-long dream of becoming a doctor was crushed.

He did report regularly to Max, he did keep up his grades, and he and Max became close friends, though Max was nine years older than Monty.

In time, Monty paid back every last dollar. And, years later, when Monty was making good money, he paid for a number of kids who couldn't afford it for them to go to college.

The one promise Monty broke?

If he were in the company of someone or a group of people putting down Max or saying derogatory or mean things about his friend, Monty would jump right in, stick up for Max, and talk about all the good things he did and all the people he had helped with no publicity.

Max Freed died in October 2010.

Upon his passing, Monty said, "Max touched so many people in his lifetime, changing lives for the better, quietly and discreetly."

When Monty would tell the story of Max Freed he'd always add, as if still amazed, "I was a perfect stranger. He was only 29. He didn't know me from a hole in the wall. And yet he put me through college. Amazing!"

# Marilyn

Before we followed Monty to New York he'd talk about Marilyn.

We were all sitting in the green room after rehearsals, and before the audience piled in for another taping of *Your First Impression*, the subject, believe it or not, was about great loves that had gotten away.

Soon it was Monty's turn.

"I had one too. While I was still in Winnipeg. It was 1944. I was going into my senior year in college. And, boy, was I in love!" He smiled, remembering, and looked at all of us to make sure he had our attention. "There was this family from LA who spent summers in Winnipeg. I met their daughter on a blind date. She was something! One date and we began to see each other every day, every night, and all the time in between. We got very serious very quickly."

He looked over at Nat Ligerman. "How's our time, Nat?"

"Plenty of time, Monty. So, what happened?"

Monty continued, "I think her father liked me but her mother didn't. One day, I think I had dinner at their house, and I was bringing dishes into the kitchen. Her mother was washing at the sink when she turned off the water and said to me, 'I've been thinking, Monty. You're a nice young man and I know how much my daughter loves you. But you're not exactly what I had in mind for her.'"

Monty responded with, "What exactly did you have in mind for her?"

'Not someone who plays records on the radio, or is the son of a butcher, or who probably doesn't have fifty dollars to his name.'

"I wish I had fifty dollars," Monty told her.

'I can't have you marry my daughter, Monty. I'm sure you understand.'

"I was crushed. But we weren't giving up just because her mother... Anyway, we secretly swore our love and allegiance to each other and we decided we were 'unofficially' engaged. The summer ended and she went back to LA with her family. I was going to look into getting a radio job in California.

"Besides my job as a fill-in at radio station CKRC, Winnipeg, I wanted to try one more time to get accepted into medical school. Surely if I became a doctor her mother would have a different opinion of me. All my senior year we corresponded with each other. In those days, before computers, we wrote letters—long, long letters.

"I think it was in April 1945, the school year ending, when I excitedly opened her latest letter to let me know the exact date she and her family were coming back to Winnipeg, when what I read destroyed me.

"She had met some guy, they had fallen in love, he had given her a big, expensive engagement ring, and they had picked out a date for the wedding. She was not coming back to Winnipeg. And this was followed up by a letter from the university saying my application for medical school was again rejected.

"Two 'Dear John' letters in a week, and I was heartbroken and resentful and confused and down-trodden. It was, without doubt, the worst time in my life... Up to then.

"How's our time, Nat?"

"Audience doesn't come in for another twenty-five minutes. Now that you've depressed us all, tell us a happy story. Tell us about Marilyn."

"It was another dreary winter in Winnipeg and my job with CKRC wasn't going anywhere, when I met with Gary Goetz, the station manager, to see about a raise."

'Monty, it's time for you to move on.'

"Move on? What the heck are you talking about?"

'Your future isn't here in Winnipeg. I think you can make it in the big time. I think it's time to try your luck in Toronto. If you stay here you'll end up like all the rest of us, fat and lazy and content and going nowhere. You're ambitious, Monty, and you're still young. Take my advice and get the hell out of here. Toronto, Monty. Toronto.'

"So I packed an old cardboard suitcase we had with all my belongings, and in February 1946 I moved to Toronto. I stayed with Norman Schnier, a cousin on my father's side.

"I made the rounds of the stations. None were interested in a nobody from Winnipeg named Monty Halparin. Except one general manager named Jack Part at radio station CHUM. He offered me $225 a month and, since nobody else wanted me, I grabbed it."

'Just one thing,' Jack Part said.

"What's that?"

'You're name.'

"What's wrong with my name?" I asked.

'It's too Jewish. Halparin is too ethnic.'

"It never bothered anybody before," I said. "If you don't count Canada's medical schools."

'It's got to be shorter. Shorter and unforgettable.'

"Like…?"

'Like Danny Kaye. One syllable. Bob Hope, one syllable. You think those were their real names?'

We both sat there thinking. He's thinking of a new name, I'm thinking, *What the heck have I gotten myself into?!*

"'Maybe,' I suggested, 'we cut my name in half.' Jack looked at me like we had just struck oil."

'I like it! Hall. Monty Hall! With two "l"s!'

"From that moment on I was Monty Hall with two "l"s.

"One day my cousin Norman tells me one of his aunts invited us to Sabbath dinner.

"'How come?' I asked."

'I want you to meet my cousin, Marilyn.'

"'How old is she?' I was curious."

'Eighteen.'

"Eighteen?!"

'She's a senior in high school.'

"I'm twenty-three. Won't that seem a little strange?"

'She's really cute. And she's a radio actress. You guys will have lots to talk about!'

I shook my head. "If there's anyone I don't want to meet it's a precocious eighteen-year-old radio actress!"

'Fine. So we'll go, have a wonderful Sabbath dinner, and come straight home.'

"So, reluctantly, I went with Norman. I met Marilyn. Norman was right. She was really cute. The house was small. She lived there with her mom, her sister, Peggy, and a maiden aunt. Her parents were separated and Marilyn was working as an actress to help support the family."

'Norman tells me you just got a job with CHUM, Mr. Hall. Congratulations.'

"Monty. Call me Monty. Norman tells me you've been acting."

'Did you listen to *Alice in Wonderland* or *Alice Through the Looking Glass*? I played Alice. The two shows have gotten me a lot of work.' She hesitated. 'And I understand you're going to be doing an early morning wake-up show.'

"I know she didn't mean it, but it sounded like she was putting me down. I'm local Toronto, she's coast-to-coast network. My salary at that time was $60 a week. And I'm twenty-three. She's eighteen and making a helluva lot more than I am.

"Maybe she didn't mean to sound precocious, but why was she sounding like the adult and me feeling like the child? "But still, she *was* cute. And we seemed to talk right along. And maybe she knew people in radio that she could introduce me to.

"So I asked her to have dinner with me.

"She said no, and she saw my look of disappointment."

'There, there,' she said. 'Don't be too upset.'

"I was being patronized! I felt like a little boy being told by his mother, 'Sorry, Son, you're just not old enough.'

"Here's where fate stepped in. Every before doing my wake-up show I ate breakfast at the same diner. There was an older man who ate there every day as well. He was general manager of Monogram Pictures, and many mornings we would chat with each other. He turned out to be, ready for this, Marilyn's father!

"When I told him about having dinner at his house, we became fast friends. He was a very nice man. And he missed his wife and daughter very much.

"I called Marilyn. 'You know your dad and I have breakfast every morning.'"

'You do?'

"He said I should ask you again to have dinner with me. He wants you to know how much he loves and misses you guys."

"We met at an Italian restaurant and I got that old feeling again. I was falling for this eighteen-year-old.

"That's when she told me she was going with this guy who was away on a business trip and that when he came home they were going to get engaged to be married."

"That's funny," I told her. "You see, you're not going to marry him. You're going to marry me!"

'Oh, really?' She smiled.

"We saw each other often after that. And we fell in love.

"I asked her to tell her other friend that their engagement was off, and she told me she already had!

"How ironic. My first love met someone else and blew me off. My forever love met me and blew off her other boyfriend.

"All because I had breakfast at the same place as her dad!

"We got married in Winnipeg. Her father walked her down the aisle. A proud man with a tear in his eye.

"On our wedding night we boarded a train going back to Toronto. I had an upper birth, she had a lower. Some honeymoon! We were in a rush to get back because Marilyn had classes and some acting jobs and I was starting a new radio show.

"The next day we got a room at the Guild Inn in Scarborough just outside of Toronto. It was the first game of the World Series. I immediately got a blank piece of paper and started drawing lines on it.

'Monty, what are you doing?'

"Making a score card. I always keep a box score."

'A what?'

"The game is about to start."

"Poor Marilyn was stunned and confused. She had no idea what I was talking about. Baseball? World Series? Box score? What happened to our honeymoon?

"The Yankees beat the Dodgers, and after the game…after the game…"

Nat Ligerman jumped in. "Monty, the audience is being seated. We better get ready."

We all got up and headed to our responsibilities.

Another taping of *Your First Impression* was about to begin.

Monty singing on the *Mildred Morey Show* (cir. 1950).

# Mr. Houston

Now, let's go back to 1949.

"Mr. Houston?"

"Yes?"

"Can I talk to you?"

"Of course. Come in. Sit down."

"My name's Monty Hall. I want to talk to you about a loan."

"Well, that's what the bank is here for. How much you looking to borrow?"

"$2,500."

"I see. And may I ask you what the loan is for?"

"I want to produce radio shows."

"Really."

"I've started my own company called Monty Hall Productions. I have a partner named Wes Cox. He's very bright. He's been editing a newspaper covering high school activities here in Toronto and he wants to go into broadcasting. My brother, Robert, helps out a little bit and I have a part-time secretary. She's practically working for free."

"And where is your office located?"

"In my apartment. For now."

"And how exactly does this production company work?"

"Wes and I, and Robert, work up ideas for shows and then I go from radio station to radio station trying to sell them."

"And, how successful have you been so far?"

"Well, so far… I mean, we really just started."

"Tell me," he looked down at a card with Monty's name on it, "Mr. Hall, what is your background?"

"I'm from Winnipeg. I got a bachelor of science degree from the University of Manitobu."

"And what was your major?"

"Chemistry and Zoology."

"Hardly a prerequisite for selling radio shows, wouldn't you agree, Mr. Hall?"

"I thought I was going to be a doctor."

"So you were going on to medical school."

"I couldn't make the quota."

"And what quota is that."

"Each school is only allowed to take in so many Jewish students. I didn't make the number."

"You really believe this?"

"I do."

"So instead of medical school, what?"

"I did a number of radio shows in Winnipeg, then decided to take my chances here in Toronto."

"And?"

"I got a job with the CBC. I did commentaries on a couple of news shows. Then I got my first national network shows. One was a quiz show and the other starred Mildred Morey."

"The comedienne?"

"You know her?"

"I listened to that show every week! And you were…?"

"I was the emcee, and I sang duets with her and—"

"You were the one she was always making fun of! You were the butt of her jokes, right?"

"That was me."

"Sunofagun! That was you!"

"Mr. Houston, we have no production companies here in Canada. The CBC creates its own shows, but the rest of the stations rely on American radio transcriptions of shows like *Arthur Godfrey* and the *Perry Como-Jo Stafford* show. There are no original Canadian shows made specifically for Canadian audiences. I want to provide these kind of shows."

"And you want $2500 to get started. Is that right?"

"Twenty-five a week for the secretary, $15 for my brother, $50 for Wes, and maybe $75 for me. And if I can find a real office for around $250 a month, that money should sustain us for two, possibly three months."

"And, Mr. Hall, what would you be putting up for collateral?"

"Collateral?"

"In case your plan falls through, how are we going to get our money back?"

"Mr. Houston, I don't have any collateral. I don't own anything."

"Humm. I see."

"All I've got is my brain and my heart. I have ideas and ambition and I will work day and night to make my production company work. I have experience in radio, I'm not a Johnny-come-lately. I am honest and I have never defaulted on a debt in my life."

Mr. Houston was quiet for a moment. Then he smiled ever-so-slightly.

"I'm not going to lend you $2,500."

Monty's heart sank.

"I'm going to lend you $5,000 instead. Three months may not be enough time. I don't want you worrying about money or putting extra pressure on yourself. It'll be enough pressure trying to sell one of your shows."

For the first time in his life Monty was speechless. What Clarence the angel was to George Bailey in *It's a Wonderful Life*, Mr. Hudson was to Monty Hall!

They moved into an office in downtown Toronto, brought in a couple of writers, and together they created a game show called *Who Am I?*

Monty would give clues in rhyme about a mystery person.

For instance: "I work with my wife. She's a real hoot. She gets the laughs. I get the boot. Who am I?"

The audience would mail in their guesses. Each show Monty would add additional clues till they would open an envelope with the correct answer and the winner would get a prize.

To sell the show, Monty took a Toronto telephone book, looked up advertising agencies, and starting with A, called every agency alphabetically.

When he got to H he found a winner! The Hennesy Agency grabbed on to *Who Am I?* and sold it to fifty-six radio stations across all of Canada. Colgate agreed to sponsor the show.

*Who Am I?* was a huge success. More stations signed up.

Hennessy paid Monty Hall Productions the paltry sum of $300 a week for the show. On one hand, Monty was glad to get it. What the heck, his first show and they were a hit! And as the emcee he was getting nationwide recognition.

On the other hand, by the time he paid his staff and rent and expenses and paid back the loan, he had little money to live on. And, at this time, Monty was married to Marilyn and they had two little kids. Monty was getting desperate.

He grew to hate Hennessy. He lied to Monty constantly, he was cheap, and he was a bully. He would promise Monty raises but the raises never came.

"I own *Who am I?*" he would say in his Irish baroque, "and if you don't like the arrangement you can quit and I'll find me another boy."

The show ran more than ten years! 1,875 performances. Hennessy made life miserable, but Monty hung in there as long as he could.

Finally, Monty accepted the fact that he had to make the break from this jerk.

With Marilyn's blessing he decided to try his luck in New York.

Leaving his wife and the two little ones, one five, the other three, Monty, frustrated and psychologically beaten down, but with head held high, got in his car and headed to the Big Apple.

YOUR FIRST IMPRESSION

# *Your First Impression*

*Your First Impression* was on NBC. It started in 1962 and ran for two years.

As previously mentioned, it's how I got my start as a writer and how Monty got his start as a producer.

And each show started with announcer Wendell Niles' opening:

"In a few moments, behind our panel you will see our famous mystery celebrity. Will it be: Joan Crawford, Betty White, Jane Mansfield, Shelly Winters, or Mary Tyler Moore. (Photos of each celebrity would be flashed on screen when their name was mentioned. And, of course, the names changed with each show.)

You'll find out when we play *Your First Impression*. Now, here's your host, Bill Layden!"

And Layden would introduce the panel who, from time to time, would be the likes of Dennis James, Rose Marie, and George Kirko. Other weeks other celebrities made up the panel.

Each panelist was given a list of five beginnings of a sentence that I had written, like "The worst part about being a celebrity is ____ ?" And the mystery celebrity, who was in a soundproof booth behind the panelists, would fill in the blank with the first thing they thought of. And only Bill Layden could hear the responses and would pass them on to the panel.

After the mystery celebrity had responded with their first impression to all 15 sentences the panel would try to analyze the responses and begin eliminating the five possibilities to guess who the mystery celebrity was.

Who created the show? Well, all these shows are eventually the collaboration of many minds, but someone had to come up with the genesis.

That man was Nat Ligerman.

I told his and Monty's story in my book, *As I Remember It: My 50 Year Career as an Award Winning Writer, Producer, and Studio Executive* (BearManor Media).

But here it is again, as Nat told it me at lunch one day.

Nat owned a laundry business in Greenwich Village in New York. Monty was one of his customers. The two couldn't be more different.

Monty was smooth, suave, urban. Nat was Brooklyn. A terrific guy, but not what you'd call a sophisticate. Monty was a college graduate, Nat a high school dropout.

But Monty was struggling, trying to get his foot in the door. All his concepts for game shows, talk shows, and/or interview shows had been rejected. Monty would tell Nat his tales of woe and Nat would feel sorry for him.

"Monty, I have an idea for a game show."

"Forget it, Nat. It's too hard. Unless you're Goodren-Todman or Merv Griffin they're not interested."

Nat insisted, "Just listen to the premise. Three panelists—"

Monty cut him off. "Nat, I got my own shows. I don't want to hear your idea."

Weeks go by. Monty's frustration, exasperation, and irritation continue. One day Monty brings some clothes in to be laundered.

"I got a meeting at NBC in a week."

Nat is happy for Monty. "Good!"

"Not good."

"Because…?"

"Because I have nothing new to show them. I've already pitched them everything I have."

Nat, timidly, "You wanna try my game?"

Monty sighed wearily. "Nat, you're a pain in the butt, but let's hear it."

So Nat pitched. "Whenever I want to cheer myself up I _____… Most important thing I learned in school was _____…" Monty listened. The show was called *Key Word*, and Monty liked the concept a lot. It wasn't a game show yet, just an idea. A gimmick.

When Monty worked out all the format to *Key Word*, Monty called Oscar Katz, head of daytime programing at CBS, to set up a meeting. Katz said he'd get back to Monty.

Nat would call Monty every day to see if Katz had called.

Finally, one day when Nat phoned Monty for the umpteenth time, Monty said, "I got a meeting with Katz for next week."

"I want to go with you."

"Not a good idea, Nat."

"Why not?"

"First of all, you have no credentials. Secondly, you might say something stupid and blow the whole meeting. And thirdly, no forget thirdly. It's just not a good idea."

"I'll sit in the corner. I won't say a word. I promise. I'll just sit and listen." By this time Nat was pleading. "I just want to be there. At a meeting. A real meeting."

Monty caved. "Alright, alright. You'll go with me."

"How should I dress?"

"You have a suit?"

"I have a suit."

"And you better shave."

"I'll buy a new blade."

So off they went to 501 Madison Avenue, the suave, sophisticated Canadian and the rough-around-the-edges dems and doz Brooklynite.

They met in Katz' office. Monty introduced Nat, who then picked a seat in a corner of the room, almost out of sight.

Katz said to Monty, "We want to proceed on *Key Word*. We'll give you office space and some money to prepare for a pilot. If that works, we'll be on the air at the first daytime opening."

"Great," says Monty.

"To get you started we'll give you $8000 as seed money."

Monty would swear the following was true.

Nat jumped out of his seat he was so excited. The money! More money than he probably made in a year! He gasped. "Eight thousand dollars!" (Remember, this is 1962.)

Katz was taken back. He thought he had insulted Nat and Monty. Then he jumped out *his* seat and angrily hollered at Nat, "Alright, make it twelve thousand!"

Now it was Monty's turn to jump up. "We'll take it. We'll take it!"

Monty grabbed Nat and the two of them left before Katz could ingest what had just happened! Out the elevator, through the lobby, and standing on Madison Avenue, Nat sheepishly turned to Monty. "Sorry, Monty, I just lost it."

Nat had just gotten them an additional $4000, and all he could do was apologize.

Whether genuine or apocryphal, Monty loved to tell that story.

For some reason never explained to me, the deal fell through. And, of course, Monty and Nat were crestfallen.

One thing about Monty, though, he would take his lumps and bounce right back up. He told Nat he'd try it on NBC. And Nat said, "Maybe you should go on your own."

Monty met with David Levy, who was vice president of programming for NBC, and pitched *Key Word*.

That evening, Monty stopped by the laundry.

Nat was on pins-and-needles.

"Well?!"

"He liked it, Nat. He really liked it."

"So now what?"

"We wait. He's got to run it by some other executives over there, and then hopefully— Let's just wait and see."

Monty and Nat shook hands, and Monty promised Nat if anything good happened Nat could sell off the laundry mat and work with Monty on the show.

So they waited. And waited.

Monty got a chance to move to Los Angeles and emcee a children's game show called *Video Village*.

So he, Marilyn, and the two kids packed up and moved to the West Coast.

And Nat figured he'd never hear from Monty again.

Months later, as Monty finished up at CBS shooting a couple of back-to-back *Video Villages*, a stagehand told him he had a call.

"Hello, this is Monty."

"Monty, it's David Levy in New York. We want to order *Key Word*."

"You do?"

"I know you got that *Video Village* going, so hire a producer and an emcee and let's see a pilot in three to four weeks."

The show they would be replacing was hosted by Bill Leyden and called *It Could Be You*. It was kind of a bastardized version of *Queen for a Day*, women telling embarrassing moments in their lives and given an appropriate gift for sharing their story. But the ratings were poor.

Bill Leyden was very good, had a good sense of humor, and daytime audiences loved him.

Monty hired Leyden to host *Key Word*, which had now changed its name to *Your First Impression*.

Wendell Niles was the announcer on *It Could* B*e You*, and Monty hired him.

And one more person. The producer of *It Could Be You* was a straight arrow, no nonsense guy named Steve Hados.

Monty took an immediate liking to his nuts-and-bolts attitude and hired him to produce.

Oh, yes, and Nat Ligerman. Monty kept his word. Nat sold the laundry mat, moved his wife and kids to Sherman Oaks in the Valley and became an associate producer.

Nat's dream of someday working in show business came true, but, I must admit, I never really figured out what Nat's job was.

But he spent a lot of time with Monty and, as different as they were, they were great friends.

The show ran two years.

# *Let's Make A Deal*

MONTY AND STEVE HADOS sat in Monty's office kicking around ideas, trying to find something they could get excited about. *Your First Impression* wasn't going to last forever, and they needed to come up with a new show.

"You know," Monty mused, "in 1947 in Winnipeg I did a radio show that was quite popular called *The Auctioneer*. We would auction things off to members of the audience or sometimes I would give someone in the audience ten dollars and tell them they can keep it or trade it for an envelope or a box that I had. Sometimes the envelope had fifty dollars, sometimes it had a stick of gum. The audience loved that part."

Steve thought on it. "You mean you could trade one gift for another, but you didn't know what the other one was?"

Monty was now getting excited. "And we would start each show with me taking a lady in the audience and offering her five dollars if she had a bus ticket in her purse, or maybe a hard-boiled egg, or maybe a clothespin."

"Let's work on it," said Steve.

I remember Monty telling a group of us how difficult it was to try-out the show.

"It wasn't your typical Q and A or stunt show. You couldn't try it out in an office, you needed an audience.

"You couldn't walk into CBS or NBC and just pitch it. It had to be seen.

"So, in order to rehearse and work out the kinks we decided to have run-throughs for any groups that would have us. Steve would call church clubs, knitting clubs, book-of-the-month clubs, health and diet clubs, senior citizen homes, anyone who would allow us to perform our show.

"And we did. Our only prizes, a rubber chicken and an envelope with a five-dollar bill. After a dozen run-throughs with these women groups we were ready to show the networks. But we didn't have a title yet. For the time being we were calling it *The Auctioneer*, but we knew we needed something catchier.

"Steve and I were walking to lunch one day when right in the middle of the street he stops, turns to me and says, 'Let's Make A Deal!'

"I got so excited that I stopped in the middle of the road, too.

"That's it, Steve! I love it!

"Like two idiots we stood in the middle of the street, oblivious of on-rushing traffic, and a bus missed us both by a half-an-inch!

"But we had our title.

"Our first run-through was for ABC.

"We rented out an auditorium, brought in 300 people for our audience, and set up three doors on the stage.

"We played the game with contestants from the audience and they were making choices and we gave away a donkey or a year's supply of pizzas and the audience was roaring with laughter even though there were no real prizes to be given out. The games were just so much fun, and the audience loved it.

"I am beside myself I am so excited. Steve and I go backstage and there's our agent and Army Grant, head of daytime for ABC.

"I'm trying not to be giddy and put on as stern a face as I can muster. 'Well, Army, what'd you think?'"

'I hated it, Monty. It's not gonna fly.'

"Didn't you hear that audience? They were howling!"

'The run-through was fine, but what are we going to do the second day?'

"I couldn't believe what he had just said. 'What do you mean what do we do the second day?! What do other game shows do? Each day is a variation of the pilot.'"

'Sorry, Monty, Steve, it's not for us.'

"I remember driving home that night more depressed than I had ever been.

"But, three weeks later we got another shot, this time with NBC. We do the show again. Still with just the rubber chicken and the envelope. Again, the audience screams and yells and gets right in it with the contestants.

"Jerry Chester, VP of programming at NBC, says to Steve and me, 'Good pilot, but what do you do for the second show?'

"I couldn't believe it. The same words. The same rejection.

"I got drunk that night. And I don't drink!

"With Jerry Chester at the run-through was Bob Aaron, head of NBC daytime television. Aaron didn't say anything because Chester was his boss. But he got word to me a couple of days later that he loved the show, saw its potential, and would work on Chester to get him to change his mind.

"He must have beat him up pretty good, because out of the blue we got the word NBC had changed their mind and would pay for a pilot.

"If I say so myself, the pilot was terrific, and NBC ordered the show."

How successful was the show?

It has played, almost consistently, at one time or another, on NBC, CBS, ABC, FOX, as well as syndicated in numerous countries throughout the world.

That's fifty-five years as of this printing...and counting!

By 1974 the show spent more than a decade as daytime television's top or near-top program.

And, also at that time, the waiting list for tickets to the show was two to three years! It was the all-time record for waiting for tickets in show-business history.

*TV Guide* listed *Let's Make A Deal* in the top twenty of all-time greatest game shows.

And all the time, Monty remembered, "But what will you do for the second show?"

# Carol Merrill

"CAROL, LET'S SEE WHAT'S behind door number three."

And for fourteen years, Carol Merrill would open yet another door.

On May 25, 1963, Carol met Monty. She was 23. She was called in to do the pilot. She had been recommended to Stefan Hatos by Bill Walsh at CBS. Carol met Monty quickly on that day because, "Monty was working and I was working because we were shooting the pilot. I didn't quite meet him that day, but I had a good feeling, a good vibe about him. I liked him immediately.

"The show's popularity built slowly. After the first 13 weeks we were thrilled that we got renewed. We made it. Every time we got renewed we'd get more and more people who showed up to want to be on the trading floor. Monty would always use my name and Jay Stewart's name. I thought it was so lovely. He used my full name."

Carol's position on the stage was in front of the curtains or boxes or behind the curtains. Monty was mostly on the trading floor with Jay Stewart, so she had less interaction during the production of the show.

"He loved telling stories. It would put a sparkle in his eyes. And, even up to his last days, if he could tell a story or a joke, he loved it. Mostly, it was about his family. He loved his family. His whole family is just fantastic people.

"Monty was so good with the contestants, he was so natural. Some of the other hosts were professional, but *Deal* became a hit because of Monty. He was responsible for how it evolved.

"He had a sparkle in his eye, what he said was always very clever. He was such a genius. Such a talented person. I liked watching Monty and Stefan Hatos work. They were so professional."

Carol loved the moments backstage when she and Monty would kid each other about how the contestants would sometimes get their names wrong. Carol said, "Monty would call me 'Cawwell Mewwell' and I would say, 'Marty Hale'. It was our little joke."

"I adored the stage hands, they used to play some tricks on me." Carol described how when they'd have a refrigerator to display as a big prize the crew would put a rubber chicken in the fridge or banana peels, "just to break me up."

"If the chicken or something like that made it onto stage at the show, Monty would just go along with it."

Carol said, "Two shows a day, back to back, sometimes we did four shows when we were doing daytime and nighttime. I began at four in the afternoon, and sometimes I'd finish at nine. We'd do rehearsal. We'd rehearse the prizes and things. We did a dry run. We had a format. After a few years I'd just be going through the paces. I did have to do a one sheet so I knew where to go. I was the only model, so if a contestant did or said something we weren't prepared for I had to be prepared to react accordingly."

Being the only model, Carol was very busy. Stefan Hatos said, "Carol is busier than a one-legged man in an ass-kicking contest."

Backstage the stage hands would say, "Just follow Carol."

"If things went wrong or something unsuspected happened, that's where Monty was a genius. He was so good at covering up things, he was so clever. If the wrong curtain was opened he'd say, 'Oh, you want to show me that one?' He'd figure his way out of it, the mistakes. He was great. The show evolved from all of our personalities: mine, Jay Stewart's, and Monty's.

"One time there was a watch that was supposed to be in a box. The watch had disappeared when it came time to do the show. Someone had lifted it, so, it was gone. Monty opened it and said, 'Whoa, there was supposed to be a watch here… We'll make sure you'll get one.'

"Monty would rarely get upset when things would go wrong. He never used foul or raunchy language. He liked humor a lot, he didn't like raunchy humor…not with me.

"One time we had an elephant on stage. The curtain opened and the elephant turned his hind side to Monty and walked away… Monty said something like, 'Oh, well, there was an elephant there.' He didn't mind things like that because he always figured out a way to get us out of it. In fact, he loved the spontaneity of the moment.

"You can't talk about Monty without mentioning Marilyn in the same breath. She was one of the most modest and sincere people in show business. Always listening to other people's stories. I adored Marilyn. She was such an inspiration. Always so tactful and respectful. She was quiet but classy and took a backseat to Monty in a sincere, modest way. She wasn't a shrinking violet, she was giving and a great listener. If she had something to say, though, she'd say it.

"One time I needed a golf outfit for when I was working on *Hollywood Squares* and Marilyn said, 'I have a golf outfit up in my attic. Come on over.'

"And not many people knew that Marilyn Hall and Sheldon Allman wrote the *Deal* theme song.

"Working with Monty was such a pleasure. For instance, he

covered things so beautifully. He was so aware of our time constraints backstage and would know if the curtain had just opened on three and I had to be on one, he would stretch it out (he would vamp). He was a genius being able to keep track of everything on stage and knowing about our time constraints. He was juggling so much, and he was so good at it.

"Another thing not many viewers knew was that I was allowed to work while pregnant. I had to face that camera straight on and I would wear dresses. They hid the pregnancy but didn't hide it. People wrote in that they suspected it, but there was no discussion of it. The show took a two month hiatus at just the right time for me to have my baby. When the show came back I had some time to get in shape for the show.

"Wherever Monty would go people would want to know more about me. They'd say, 'What's Carol doing?' He got a kick out of that.

"Celebrities were constantly visiting our set. Dean Martin would call me 'legs'. I liked that.

"Johnny Carson came backstage one evening. I was over at door number one. The curtain was closed and I was about to model a home entertainment center, and in comes Johnny Carson. I had never met him. He says, 'How do you do this?' Then, the curtain opened and there's Johnny Carson talking to me. He surprised Monty and the audience. It was one of the very few times Monty was speechless!

"One of the last times I talked to Monty was on his birthday in 2014. He answered the phone! I said, 'You were an inspiration.' He said, 'Is that anything like perspiration?' I said, 'With perspiration, you get more toxins out.' He laughed, he really liked humor."

Carol's last show on *Deal* was December 22, 1976. Fourteen years. Not a bad run.

# Hank Koval

I'VE GOTTA TELL YOU about Hank Koval. Unlike *Let's Make A Deal*, where audiences would write in for tickets two and three years in advance, hardly anyone ever wrote in for tickets for *Your First Impression*.

Hank's job was to fill those seats for every single performance.

He would contact churches, synagogues, hospitals, schools, women's clubs, men's clubs, anywhere he could bus in a group to make sure there was a full house.

Then there was the paddle. Made of plain wood, it was larger than a fraternity paddle but shorter than an oar.

It was Hank's and he carried it everywhere on the set of *Your First Impression*. And on the paddle he collected the autographs of every celebrity that ever appeared on the show. A literal who's who of movie stars, television performers, singers, and comics. Some collector would probably pay a lot of money for that paddle. I wonder where it is now?

Hank then went on to *Let's Make a Deal* and was there for every one of the 4,500 shows.

Because the audience was self-perpetuating, Hank had other jobs. He would check the props and prizes and take photos of the "zonks." He was also in charge of the money. He'd hold on to $1,000 in cash for every show.

The contestants would not go home with the money. Hank would collect the cash at the end of the show and cut the winners checks.

Hank remembered that Monty didn't like to rehearse. He wanted the show to have a certain spontaneity. Hank agreed that no emcee was as quick-witted or as glib as Monty, who always wanted to meet the contestants unrehearsed and fresh.

"Monty knew the structure of each show. He knew what deals were coming up. He knew the script and he'd go over the lead lines on the cue cards, and he'd know when we'd need to break for commercials, but he wouldn't rehearse any of the acts.

"The show was truly 'live', and Monty would ad-lib and come up with cute and clever repartee for every situation.

"When Monty would come off stage I was in charge of reminding him what was coming next. What deals were next, what aisle to go to, what section, who to call on, and I'd give him the money.

"The writers would choose people or couples beforehand for the big acts. They were always looking for contestants that they thought Monty would work well with, depending on the acts.

"Monty wasn't fond of people who would scream at him to get his attention. If you screamed you were guaranteed not to be picked.

"There are many stories about how the costumes began. Well, this is the *real* story. When people would line up outside of NBC, this one guy showed up all the time dressed as the Jolly Green Giant. He drove everybody crazy always pleading to be picked.

"Finally, one of the writers chose him just to get rid of the guy. He got to be on the show in that costume because that's all he had to wear. They put him on the trading floor and he got his two minutes of fame on television. What he did was open up the flood gates, because then *everybody* started showing up in costume. All because of the Jolly Green Giant. And that's the true story.

"Here are my two favorite Monty Hall stories. One happened on the show, the other had nothing to do with the show.

"Monty was with this woman who was dressed like a baby. He offered her $50 if she had a nipple (a baby pacifier). And, she had it, so Monty gave her the $50. Then, he said that if she had another nipple he'd give her $100. Well, she began to take her top off. Monty stopped her right away and gave her the $100.

"The other story involves Monty's wife. Marilyn had to take her car in for service. When it was ready to go Monty said he'd pick it up for her. He got to the mechanics and realized that he had two cars with him.

"Well, Monty drove Marilyn's car for one block. He parked it, got out, and walked back to get his car. He then drove his car two blocks, parked it, got out and walked back.

"He did that all the way home! Got two cars home one block at a time.

"The women were always kissing Monty, and many times getting lipstick on his face. He'd come off during a break and I'd take out my handkerchief and wipe the lipstick off his face, then I'd put the handkerchief back in my pocket. Well, one time my wife was doing my laundry and pulled out this handkerchief with lipstick all over it. She just had to ask me about that! Monty got the kisses and I got in trouble!

"And finally, some random thoughts about Monty.

"Monty was easy to get along with. He always had a spirit of friendliness that permeated throughout the entire staff. He was the perfect host for *Let's Make a Deal.*

"Monty took you on your word. Trust was very important to him. Monty and Stef Hatos did not have a partnership contract. They had no legal paperwork. It was just a handshake.

"Monty was very religious, yet he hardly ever talked about it. But he and Marilyn would

always have a lot of people over for Passover. I was a gentile, but I was invited many times. He'd always have a rabbi there for the service. But you never felt like an outsider. I will always have nice, warm, remembrances of Passover at the Hall's."

# Jay Stewart

ALL THIS INFORMATION ON Jay Stewart comes from research, as he died in 1989 before I started this book.

While Jay was an announcer on numerous game shows, he was certainly best known as Monty's side-kick on *Let's Make a Deal.* He assisted Monty on stage on a number of the acts and also would don silly costumes as "zonk" prizes.

Monty called Jay "The best second banana you ever found in your life." And, "We had a very, very good feeling between us. Jay's booming voice, his bubbly personality endeared him to millions."

Few knew that one of Jay's daughters had committed suicide in 1981.

It was said that Jay suffered from severe depression and insufferable back pain for years. Alcohol was a salve, but it wasn't a cure.

In 1989 Jay Stewart stunned friends and colleagues when he died of a self-inflicted gunshot wound. He was 71.

# The Costumes

WHEN *LET'S MAKE A Deal* started audiences showed up nicely dressed, women in dresses, men in sports jackets or sweaters.

But in the second week a woman, hoping to be picked, showed up at the studio with a sign: 'Roses are red, violets are blue, I came here to deal with you.'

Monty read the sign and picked the lady to be a contestant.

By the next week *everybody* showed up with signs, all thinking that was the way to get picked!

A week after that someone came in wearing a funny hat. Then came the costumes. There were Tarzans, Batmen, clowns, devils, Ruth Buzzi look-a-likes, and women in shoulder pads and helmets all hoping for their moment with Monty.

NBC called for a meeting.

"Monty, what are you going to do about all these crazy people showing up like they just escaped a loony bin?"

"What do you mean what are we going to do?"

"We can't have 300, 400 adults every day wandering around NBC dressed like Halloween rejects!"

"Why not? We've got the most colorful show on television. It adds quite a flavor to the show. It truly becomes the peoples' show."

NBC had no answer. They just warned Monty not to turn the

show into a costume contest and not to just pick people for the outlandish costumes they wore.

To play against that, Monty even picked contestants who were not wearing costumes. He continued to just pick people at random.

Monty had two rules that the staff had to obey. One, don't let anyone into the studio carrying a weapon—even if it's fake.

Tell the "Arab Potentates" no machetes. Tell the "escaped convicts" no knives. Tell the "Columbo" look-a-likes no guns. And tell the "evils" no pitchforks.

The second rule. Absolutely no men dressed as babies in diapers! Monty told his staff if they let any man in a diaper onto the trading floor they would be fired! Not the diaper man, the staff member.

But Monty loved the costumes. Some, he said, were brilliant. Even the ones that were awful Monty thought were brilliant.

Monty was right when he said *Let's Make a Deal* is the peoples' show.

# The Prizes

Critics panned it.

"It brings out the worst in people."

"Pure greed."

"It's gambling, and gambling is sinful."

"Cupidity."

"They would wait up to three years for tickets to dress up like idiots, stand in a long line outside the studio for maybe three hours in the sun, jump up and down and plead when the writers would come out to pick possible contestants, wave home-made signs with cutsie, stupid sayings, and finally, when they get into the studio, would scream as the emcee appeared.

And then if they were picked to be a contestant they'd scream again. And jump up and down. And then as their first prize would be revealed they would scream once more. And again jump up and down.

Now the emcee would say they could trade that prize for what's behind one of three doors or in one of three boxes or behind one of three curtains.

It may be a "zonk," a gag gift, or it may be an all-expense paid trip around the world. The contestant would quiver with excitement. Take the $1000 she was just given or trade it in for a sway-back horse? A year's supply of turnips? Or that around-the-world trip or a flashy new car or a boat or yacht, or…or…?

Of course she's going to take the chance. She didn't wait three years for tickets, stand in the hot sun for three hours, and dress like a totally embarrassed fool for a measly $1,000!

She guesses door number one.

The emcee now entices her by revealing the prize behind door number two, one of the two doors she didn't pick. Of course it's a "zonk," a couple of full-grown cows.

"Now," he asks, "you want to stick with door number one or try your luck with door number three?"

Again she would quiver, procrastinate, ponder. And, egged on by the smiling emcee, she would make a decision. She would know she would either scream again, or if she got a year's supply of lemonade be disappointed but smile. If she chooses the wrong door, greed had done her in. She could have kept the $1000. But if she chooses right, more screaming, more jumping.

Win or lose, the audience loved every heart-wrenching, heart-pounding moment. Three hundred and fifty audience members would sit in the bleachers of the studio.

Ten or twelve will actually get on the show. The rest scream and yell for those who make it.

The name of the show, of course, is *Let's Make a Deal.* The host for over 4,500 of those shows was Monty Hall.

No emcee could adlib as constantly or as quick-wittedly based on the contestant's choices as Monty.

He and partner Steve Hades created the show in 1963 and it aired on all three networks at different times during the next 28 years with two breaks, one from 1977 to 1980, the other from 1981 to 1984. Monty retired in 1991 and Wayne Brady became the present emcee.

Now, about those prizes.

Monty said they would pay for the expensive prizes. The minor gifts were given to the production company for plugs for their products.

Monty swore they never got cut-rate prizes or free big-money gifts from any company.

"I buy my cars at a dealership," Monty said, "and my TV sets at a discount appliance store. A lot of these charities think we can have hundreds of free cars delivered whenever we snap our fingers. Not so."

Monty told of the time he spoke at a memorial luncheon in Palm Springs. After the lunch the president of the organization asked him if he could get them a color TV set for their bazaar.

Monty told her he had nothing to do with the prizes they gave away on the show and that he personally had no connections.

But she insisted.

A few days later she wrote Monty asking when their TV would be delivered.

Monty wrote her back, "Sorry, I just cannot help you."

A few days after that she called. "Have you found a TV for us yet?"

Monty was getting exasperated. Again he told her he couldn't help her.

The end of the story? Nope.

She had the chutzpah to call Monty yet again!

Monty tried not to lose it.

"Look, I have a color TV in my office. If you can send someone over here in the next hour you can have it!"

And she did. And they hauled Monty's TV set away!

End of story now? Nope.

A few days later, another woman called Monty.

"Mr. Hall, I'm president of a charity group in Desert Hot Springs. I heard that you're giving away television sets and I was wondering if…"

# Wanting More

WITH THE SUCCESS OF *Let's Make a Deal*, and particularly the popularity of the host, many doors were suddenly open to Monty, and he wanted to step through all of them.

Be guest star on a situation-comedy? Monty did it.

Star in a TV movie? Monty couldn't wait.

Guest on the late-night show? Monty was willing and ready.

You would think Monty could write his own ticket.

Not so.

If Monty had a big ego, fate, television, and Las Vegas knocked that ego right out of him. And because of the disappointments Monty suffered from a bit of an inferiority complex, that's true.

I remember him saying, "When you're a performer and you're doing a game show you feel that you're playing in the minor leagues and you feel you should be playing in the major leagues even though you're a .400 hitter in the minors. All you really want is a chance to bat in the majors."

He wanted to be more than just a game show host. He wanted to play with the big boys in the big leagues with the Mike Wallaces, the Johnny Carsons, or even the Regis Philbins.

He came close. Oh, so close.

Monty got the word around he would love to do a talk show, either day time, night time—frankly, any time.

He knew he had more in himself besides the game show. "I know I have the ability to adlib, to talk right along, and the intelligence to do many, many more things with my life."

Monty knew while he loved to sing he wasn't a great singer, and while he loved to act he knew he probably wasn't a great actor.

What he was, was a communicator. And he knew he could do a damn good talk show.

So, while he was doing *Let's Make a Deal* Johnny Carson had an argument with NBC and walked off *The Tonight Show*.

Monty got a call from an executive at NBC. "We want you to take over for Johnny Carson. We don't know how long he'll be out, but we want you to start right away. You available?"

Monty was in shock. "Yes, yes I'm available."

The same executive called Monty back just a couple of hours later.

"Monty, I'm sorry, but it's not going to work."

"Huh?"

"I checked with Carson. Gave him your name. And Carson said no. I don't know why, Monty, he just didn't want you to replace him."

Need I tell you how Monty felt?

Another time in 1974 Monty got a call from CBS.

"Monty, we're replacing *The Dinah Shore Show* and want to know if you'd be available to do a 90-minute across-the-board afternoon talk show.

Monty knew it meant walking away from Steve Hados and *Let's Make a Deal.*

Hados always hated the fact that Monty was putting down *Let's Make a Deal* by letting everyone know he was looking to move onward and upward.

It's probably the only major disagreement the two ever had.

Monty called Grant Tinker at NBC.

"Grant, what should I do? I've waited for a talk show, literally, all my life. Now they're offering me an hour-and-a-half, five-days a week. What do you think?"

"Would you have to leave *Let's Make a Deal*?

"I'd have to."

"Let me ask you this, Monty. How big is your ego?"

Monty thought. "Not that big."

So Monty turned down the one job he always wanted. He just couldn't give up the game show that made him rich and famous. His ego said "take it," but his responsibility was to Hados, the staff, the network, and himself.

Did Monty regret the decision he made? Years later he said he got over the hurt, but when he was at the crossroads of his career, rather than take the road less traveled he chose to go back.

In 1977 *Let's Make a Deal* had gone off the air and Monty got a call from Metro Media. They wanted to create a talk show especially for Monty.

They canvassed their stations to get their feelings and to see how many of the stations would buy the show.

The word comes back: "Get a real host. Monty Hall's only a game show emcee."

"Hello, Monty. We decided to go in a different direction. We think we're going to hire the Captain and Tennille. Sorry, Monty, you're the best game show host on television, but I'm afraid that may be your cross to bear. You know how this town loves to label people. Best game show host on television ain't a bad label. Sorry, Monty."

Again, another "Sorry, Monty."

# Las Vegas

1971.

The billboard in front of the Sahara Hotel announced the next attraction. Carl Ballentine, The Kids Next Door, and in huge ten-foot tall letters above the other names: MONTY HALL.

Maybe he'd never have his own network talk show. Or even a variety show, but somehow Monty was headlining a main room Las Vegas extravaganza! He was very excited, convinced his career was about to take a turn.

"And if I bomb, I always have *Let's Make a Deal* to fall back on," he told Jay Stewart, his announcer.

Carl Ballantine did a comedy-magic act. He played Ed Sullivan numerous times and was a regular on Earnest Borgnine's *McHale's Navy.*

The Kids Next Door were a young, fresh-faced, attractive, talented singing group.

It looked like a nice, family-friendly show for the Vegas tourists who idolized Monty on television.

After many rehearsals with Ballentine and the Kids, they were ready for opening night. Of all the telegrams Monty got in his dressing room, his favorite read: "Imagine ham from a kosher butcher shop."

As he sat in his dressing room he thought back to the variety shows he used to do in Winnipeg. Local tap dancers. Local singers. Raising money for the local Boys Club, or Girl

Scouts, or veterans' clubs.

He thought about the biggest names in show business who starred in Vegas, some on the very same stage he was about to go on.

"Ten minutes, Mr. Hall. Good luck."

He thought to himself that he wished the hotel people hadn't insisted on his doing any of *Let's Make a Deal.* He wanted to get away from the game show. Not remind the audience that's who he was. He was Monty Hall, the song and dance man. The guy who told funny stories, played stooge for Ballantine's silly magic tricks, did soft shoe with The Kids Next Door.

That's how he wanted to be remembered.

The show went on with hardly a flaw.

Friends and family came backstage and congratulated Monty, Carl Ballantine, and the Kids.

And then the reviews came in.

Ralph Pearl, critic for the *Las Vegas Sun*, said that while Monty was personable and charming, his show was bad and boring, and there's nothing more boring to cafe-goers than to watch other cafe-goers win goodies.

John L. Scott in the *LA Times* said that Monty was a genial master of ceremonies, glib and personable, but Scott predicted a not-so-great future for Monty as a song and dance man.

Other reviewers said family-friendly shows are fine around Easter and Christmas, but the high rollers expect more pizzazz from their Vegas shows.

Twenty-six more shows to go. Two a night for two full weeks.

They slashed the show, taking out most of Monty's opening monologue, taking out many of the songs and dances and putting in more of—the one thing Monty didn't want to do—*Let's Make a Deal.*

They turned Monty into the one thing he didn't want to be. They turned him into a game-show emcee.

"I should have fought them," sighed Monty years later. "But I didn't."

The two-week run dragged on slowly, audiences filling less than half the room.

Monty, of course, was embarrassed and dejected and couldn't wait to get back to LA, back to his huge, comfortable home in Beverly Hills, back to Marilyn and his children, and back to *Let's Make a Deal.*

# Monty's Second Disaster

DID MONTY CRAWL BACK to the comfort of his game shows and give up on his dream of being a song-and-dance man? Not Monty.

He needed a second chance. And he got it.

Monty made a deal with ABC to do a variety show special. Two young producers were brought in to help Monty create the special.

Art Fisher and Neal Marshall were a hot team. Art created *The Monkees Special* and the *Andy Williams Special,* which got him *The Andy Williams* weekly show and then the *Sonny and Cher Show.*

Monty loved their enthusiasm and loved their idea for his special.

"We'll give them a Monty Hall they've never seen before." Fisher was beaming as he spoke.

"You, Monty, are going to travel around the state of California. We'll put you in Chinatown in San Francisco, have you go deep-sea fishing off of Monterey, put you on an Indian reservation outside Palm Springs, or a ranch where you'll ride with real cowboys, and then doing the mariachi in a Mexican town outside San Diego.

"You'll talk to the natives. Sing and dance and fish with them. If they go to some festival or perform some traditional ritual, you'll be right there with them."

"Sounds great." Monty was genuinely excited. "Have you got a name for this show?"

"We'll call it…ready? We'll call it *Monty Hall: Of, for, and by the People*."

Monty gushed. "Let's do it!"

Monty loved the concept and the title so much he was sure, instead of a one-shot, the show would become a weekly series. And, he visualized, in coming weeks they would visit cities and landmarks all over the country, and in the second year, all over the world.

Monty was busy out of town while Fisher and Marshall put the hour special together. Monty would call in daily and the boys would tell him everything was steamrolling ahead and they would easily make their air date. Once he called in and Art, always the enthusiast, told Monty the title of the show had been changed.

Monty didn't like the sound of that. "What's wrong with the title we had?"

"Too bland. Too boring."

"And the new title is…?"

"*Monty Hall's Smokin', Stoken' Fire Brigade!*"

Monty was stunned.

Fisher bubbled with excitement. "Don't you love it?!"

"I… I don't—"

"We're gonna put you on the back of a five engine and ride the streets of California. I mean, will that get attention or what?!"

Monty, meekly, "I thought the original idea of me being with people and —"

"Let me handle it, Monty. This is going to be terrific. Trust me, this show will be a big winner!"

It only got worse for Monty. He had lost all control over the show. It was now Fisher's show and the whole original concept that Monty loved had now been thrown out the window.

Remember earlier I had said that I learned from Monty to never take a sabbatical when you have a show on the air? Or in this case, about to be put on the air. In this ego-infested industry there's always someone ready to take control away from you.

So, instead of Monty being a man of the people, he was now a fireman driving around on the back end of a fire truck with sirens blaring!

Monty asked to see a script. They told him not to worry.

"Don't I need to approve the script?"

"Monty, stop worrying. We've got it handled."

Monty should have been stronger. He wasn't.

In truth, Fisher didn't think much of Monty's talents. He thought Monty was a mediocre singer at best and should stick to his emceeing game shows. To protect Monty he surrounded him with celebrities, comedians, and singers. When the show was taped the guest stars overwhelmed Monty. Not only that, but Fisher spent the majority of each shooting day placating the celebrities. Monty would always be last to perform, and in most cases they had to rush through his song or his routine before losing the light. There was no time to reshoot. No time to make Monty's part better.

Also, on many days after wrapping the day's shooting Monty would be taken by helicopter to the studio to tape two *Let's Make a Deal* shows.

When the variety show was being edited, again the boys wouldn't let Monty participate.

When Monty finally saw a screening of *Monty Hall's Smokin', Stroken' Fire Brigade*, two days before airing, he was totally depressed. He saw his voice was tired, strained, and had cracked a few times on notes he had to reach for. Fisher "protected" Monty with lots of slapstick humor that wasn't funny.

"It's no good," he told Fisher.

"You're wrong, Monty. It's terrific."

Monty was not wrong. The show got crucified. The critics agreed the first half, where Monty rode around in the fire truck, was downright awful. "Embarrassing," some critics said.

While the second half was somewhat better, who knew? No one in their right mind would have hung around to watch it!

Monty shouldered the blame for the fiasco.

"My biggest mistake was letting Fisher take over for me. I should have insisted we stay with the original concept. From the moment I let them change the title, the show was lost.

"I don't blame Fisher. He got the show he wanted. It just wasn't the show I wanted. I should have been tougher, insisting on my rights as the star and owner of the show.

"I should have been. But I wasn't."

# The Dean Martin Roast

ON DECEMBER 12, 1973, Dean Martin's popular *Celebrity Roast* on NBC honored Monty Hall.

All the shows in the series were shot at the MGM Grand and some of the guests on the dais that night were two great movie star-dancers, Gene Kelly and Donald O'Conner; television personality and fellow Canadian, Art Linkletter; funny man, Jack Carter; and the former middleweight boxing champion, Rocky Graziano.

Here, now, is the transcript of the best parts of that show. Remember, it's a roast, and it's all in fun and all at Monty's expense.

## DEAN MARTIN

I'm not asking you to laugh or applaud during this roast, just stay awake. I know you may be asking why we're honoring Monty Hall. Remember, I asked first!

I don't know too much about Monty. I know he was born in Manitoba, Canada, and he's about as exciting as his home town! Manitoba is so square you can't buy a brassiere without a prescription!

Monty was destined to host quiz shows, even in Manitoba. He'd go up to strange girls and say, "Let's Make a Deal".

## ROCKY GRAZIANO

(Referring to Monty)

I don't even know who this guy is. They gave this guy a star on Hollywood Blvd. Even Dean (Martin) doesn't have a star on Hollywood Blvd. Of course he doesn't need one. He just lives there, himself!

First they tried to put Monty's footprints in front of Graumann's Chinese Theater, but Monty's so dull he made no impression! In closing, let me say Monty's show has put more people asleep than I did with my right hook! Thank you.

## DONALD O'CONNER

It's great to be here tonight. Of course there's some critics who disparage *Let's Make a Deal.* They say the whole show is based on greed. But they're wrong.

Greed is Frank Sinatra asking a lady of the evening if she gives green stamps.

But I don't want to criticize you, Monty. *Let's Make a Deal* is a terrific show. And from the bottom of my heart there's only one thing I can wish for you. When you go home to your wife tonight you find a strange man behind curtain number two!

## DEAN MARTIN

Monty, a lot of your friends couldn't be here tonight, but they sent a number of wires and I'd like to read a few right here.

The first one is from a Mary Tracey. It says, "Dear Monty, I've been standing in line for your show for eighteen months. I'm dressed as an ear of corn. I have fallen in love with the man in front of me who is dressed as a lima bean. Please get us on the show fast because we're expecting a little succatash!"

Here's one from Attorney General John Mitchell, who was convicted for conspiracy, obstruction of justice, and perjury, and was sent to prison for his role in the Watergate break-in and coverup. "Dear Monty, I would love to come on your show and win an oven so I can stick my head in it!"

## GENE KELLY

I love Monty Hall. I especially love the way people dress up with big orange feet and long green tails and purple wigs. Of course, Dean sees those without even turning on his TV!

Monty has three beautiful children, that's true. He had a fourth but he traded it away for a year's supply of dog food and a microwave oven!

There's another reason the *Dean Martin Comedy Hour* is honoring Monty Hall tonight... We couldn't get Peter Marshall!

## ART LINKLETTER

As everyone knows, those of us in television live and die with the Nielson ratings. The ratings that tell us how many people we have watching.

There's another very important rating. ABC recently did a demographic rating of Monty Hall's program to show you the *kind* of people who watch. What makes it popular. They discovered *Let's Make a Deal* appeals to almost any kind of person you can think of.

For instance, insomniacs like it, it puts them to sleep even in the afternoon! People with cardiac conditions love it because their doctors advise them no kinds of excitement under any conditions! The Rotor Rooter man likes it, they like to see someone else going down the drain for a change! And the Gay Liberation Group likes *Let's Make a Deal* because it proves there's no fun in being straight!

Monty's wife likes it because for thirty minutes every day she knows where he is!

There's only one group, one descending group, the manufacturers of Bandini fertilizer, because they feel it's strictly unfair competition!

## JACK CARTER

Monty Hall is the king of the menopause set. I was in the men's room with Monty earlier. He stood there for hours. He couldn't make up his mind. He couldn't decide to go behind door one, door two, or door three! By the time he made up his mind it was too late!

Did you ever watch that idiotic show? It's embarrassing. People get dressed like weirdos, and they come down there hoping to win five dollars and a box of pitted olives! Last week a guy showed up as a meatloaf. Monty got so excited he ate him!

He had a couple of kids on last week, five-year-olds. They were dressed as a bride and groom. Monty said, "Hi there. You're so cute. What are your names?" The little girl says, "Mr. and Mrs. Smith." Monty asked, "Would you like to be on my show?" And the little girl said, "We can't. My husband just wet his pants."

When Monty graduated he left Manitoba, Milwaukee, Manischewitz, and joined the Royal Canadian Air Force. When Queen Elizabeth visited Canada she stopped in front of Monty and asked him what he did before he joined the Air Force.

He said, "I was a photographer, Your Majesty."

"Strange," she said. "I have a brother-in-law who's a photographer."

He said, "That's strange. I have a brother-in-law who's a queen!"

## DEAN MARTIN

Here he is now, the king of the game shows, Mr. Monty Hall.

## MONTY HALL

I don't know why I did this. I could have done a bar mitzvah in Cairo.

Rocky Graziano, you won more than 70 fights, half of them with policemen! I remember Rocky in action. Some of the most graceful dives I've ever seen!

And Donald O'Conner. Remember him from the *Francis the Mule* pictures? Proving even in Hollywood a jackass can become a star. And the mule didn't do so bad either! And I'll bet it's not easy dancing in those orthopedic shoes!

And Gene Kelly, I loved you and Frank Sinatra on that tribute to senility you guys did. Actually, Gene and Frank really didn't dance on that show, they stood in one place and somebody moved the scenery up and down!

And Mr. Art Linkletter, I have great respect for my elders! I couldn't help thinking about your old show *People are Funny*. You're not one of them.

And to Jack Carter, who really turned the crowd on tonight. Jack came up from nothing, and he brought it with him!

And a special thanks to Dean Martin. He's here tonight whether he knows it or not! You know I made my singing debut on his show last year, and Dean is amazing. He never shows up for rehearsals. You have to do everything for him. Even on his recent honeymoon!

DEAN MARTIN

Oh, no. I was there. I didn't do good, but I was there!

MONTY HALL

In closing, I want to say, at first I wasn't sure I wanted this "honor," but my wife, Marilyn, said, "If you can suffer the slings and arrows of the greats of show business and not get upset it'll be a great step forward. And tomorrow I'm gonna take a great step forward and look for a new wife!

Sincerely, my deepest thanks to all of you people, and I'll be talking about it for months. Even if it's just to my psychiatrist!

## The Daytime Emmy Awards

There have been dozens of tributes to Monty over the years.

Among the tributes was the Lifetime Achievement Award, presented to Monty at the Daytime Emmy Awards in 2013.

The presenter was Wayne Brady, who had replaced Monty on *Let's Make a Deal.*

Here's an excerpt from Monty's acceptance speech.

MONTY HALL

Thank you. Receiving this award is very, very nice. This presentation is by my adopted son, Wayne Brady. You are my adopted son.

WAYNE BRADY

Thank you.

MONTY HALL

And, I'm very, very happy to have him on board. Now, Wayne, having done 6,000 shows and produced another 2,000, there's a lot of people I could thank tonight, but we don't have the time. But I would like to acknowledge all the networks that put me on the air and the viewing public that kept me there!

There's one person to note. Twenty-seven years ago, my wife, Marilyn Hall, won an Emmy. Twenty-seven years ago.

For twenty-seven years people would come to my house, see the Emmy and say, "Is that yours, Monty?" And I'd say, "No." But very proudly I'd say, "That's Marilyn's."

But now, with this presentation, when they come to my house I'll be able to say, "This one is hers and this one is mine!

Among other tributes, in 1973 Monty received a star on the Hollywood Walk of Fame; in 2000, a Golden Palm Star on the Palm Springs, California Walk of Stars; and in 2002, he was inducted into Canada's Walk of Fame.

Now, part of the presentation to Monty was supposed to be a video made by Monty's daughter, Joanna Gleason, honoring her father.

Unfortunately, the host of the award show, Wayne Brady, went off script in order to heap his personal feelings in praise of Monty and the show began running long. It was decided, by the director, to cut Joanna's tribute to her father.

Here, in its entirety are the words of Joanna Gleason, as never seen or heard on television.

## JOANNA GLEASON

What's behind door number one, two, or three has become a permanent part of American culture. The contestants could win or they could lose or they could get zonked, you never knew what was going to happen.

And the man who created and hosted the daily doses of excitement was Monty Hall.

My father, Monty Hall, and his partner, Stephan Hados, came up with the idea for *Let's Make a Deal* in 1963. It became an instant hit on NBC, and later helping ABC to become number one in daytime.

Although that success came quickly, my father's journey to *Let's Make a Deal* was anything but easy or fast.

He grew up in Winnipeg, Canada. The family had little money. Monty worked at my grandfather's butcher shop for years.

In a remarkable twist of fate, financial support arrived in the form of a wonderful benefactor. Monty got a chance to go to college. It was there he fell in love with broadcasting.

After graduation he worked a number of Canadian stations as an announcer and a sports personality.

But my father has always been a driven person in whatever he did. And his career was no exception.

Our family moved to New York in the late 50's to be with him as he hosted the game show *Video Village*.

When the show moved to Los Angeles, so did we.

It was there that Monty started pitching ideas.

He joined with a good friend, Stephen Hados, and together they came up with the concept and title, *Let's Make a Deal*.

When contestants started showing up in costumes so they'd get Monty's attention the show's ratings went through the roof!

With that success firmly established, the Hados-Hall team went on to produce many other game show formats, including *Split Second*, which ran on ABC for three years.

But the story of my father, Monty Hall, doesn't rest solely with his television shows. He has managed to raise, through his efforts, to raise for charity over one billion dollars for the many charities, telethons, and events he's hosted and supported over the last sixty years.

As a result, his native land awarded him the Order of Canada for his humanitarian work in Canada and other nations of the world.

The kid from Winnipeg has never forgotten how he was helped by someone reaching out and changing his life.

This Lifetime Achievement Award is a fitting tribute to someone who has given so much to our business and our culture.

Monty asked Wayne on the air when were they going to show the piece that Joanna made. He was terribly disappointed when the piece had to be cut.

# Jack Rusen

*MONTY'S COUSIN, JACK RUSEN, a doctor in Winnipeg, in his own words, told us these stories about Monty.*

When one of our uncles, who was a physician, died, Monty established a bursary at the University of Manitoba in the faculty of medicine in our uncle's name. It always bothered him that this was done after our uncle's death, and that our uncle never got to appreciate what had been done. So the following year Monty established a bursary in the faculty of dentistry in my father's name, in the faculty of law in his brother's name, in the faculty of medicine in my name, and in the faculty of science in his own name. He said he wanted to do this while we were all alive.

He had a great way with children.

On one visit to Winnipeg while I was a medical resident at the hospital, I told Monty about a nine-year-old boy who had been in an accident and was a quadriplegic who watched his show religiously and loved it. He said let's go now and visit him with him. I said, "How do you want me to get you in the door?" He said, "Just get the child to mention my name and I'll do the rest."

Well, I went into the child's room and said to him, "Who is your favorite TV star?" He replied, "Monty Hall." ... And Monty walked around the corner and asked, "Did somebody call my name?"

The boy, who was paralyzed from the neck down, just about jumped out of bed! Monty spent a good hour with him doing close-up magic, telling stories, and entertaining him. He was always so generous with his time when it came to children, especially if they were in the hospital.

I'm sure you know the story of Max Freed, who was the person who funded Monty's university education. That story has been widely published. Max Freed was just nine years older than Monty, which makes it even more remarkable that a man of 28 years old would be inclined to give money to a stranger to allow him to go to University.

Max and Monty maintained a friendship for the rest of their lives.

Just before Max died, at the age of 100, they visited together and Monty said to Max, "Max, you gave me a life." And Max replied, "No Monty, you gave me a life."

As you well know, Monty did countless numbers of appearances for charity, and he never charged any of the organizations a nickel for any of his appearances.

He never liked the expression "giving back." He said the expression implied something had been taken, which was not the case. He believed in charity for its own sake, and felt it was incumbent on everyone to be mindful of being charitable and doing good for others.

He loved doing crossword puzzles. He did the *New York Times* crossword puzzle in ink, but didn't start until Thursday because he thought Monday, Tuesday, and Wednesday were too easy. And he almost always completed them as well.

He was overly generous with everybody but did not overindulge himself. For many years my father and I and Monty's brother, Bob, would spend a week with Monty in Palm Springs playing golf.

After one of those games we came back to the house to find the telephone message machine blinking, and he played the message on speaker. It was his partner, Stephan Hados, telling him that he was holding a seven-figure check from Germany which represented the sale of *Let's Make a Deal* tapes which were being dubbed into German, and that he hoped Monty's share was enough to cover his losses on the golf course.

We had not had lunch at that time, so I, being the youngest, was given the task of driving to the store to get some eggs, coffee, and other food items. As I was leaving Monty called me to come with him into the kitchen, where there was a large wicker basket filled with coupons.

I couldn't believe it. I said, "Are you telling me that you save coupons?" He said, "Yes. It doesn't make sense, does it? Take today.

I wake up in the morning, have a wonderful day on the golf course, and come back to find I have a chunk of money that I didn't have when I teed off." I said, "No, it doesn't." And after pausing for five seconds or so he went back to the basket and found a $.35 coupon.

He was always trying to do for others. It always had been his dream to have a large compound where all the family could come to vacation at once. That never happened, but he did have a home in Palm Springs in addition to the one that he kept for himself and Marilyn that my parents and my aunt and uncle and many other members of our family, including my wife and I, vacationed at for many, many years.

He left nothing out. It came with a car, full golf privileges at the golf course, and movie passes for the theater. He just could not do enough for his family.

Before there was a Dean Martin and Jerry Lewis there was a comedy team in the 1940s and 1950s named Bud Abbott and Lou Costello. They had their own radio show, made movies, and later appeared on early television. Bud was the straight, befuddled, and confused comic. They were an enormous success, and Monty remembered them on radio and probably saw a half-a dozen of their feature films. They had one routine, "Who's on First," that to this day remains a classic and is probably the best known comedy skit of all time in the United States.

Lou died in 1959. Bud hung on without him, but by 1974 Bud was penniless, ill, and living in a nursing home.

The story goes, he was playing cards one day when he announced, "I have to leave the game. Sorry, guys."

One of the other players was concerned. "What's the matter, Bud, not feeling well?"

"I'm fine. I mean as fine as someone with cancer can be. *Let's Make a Deal* is on and I never miss the show. I love watching how that Monty Hall works."

Bud would go back to his room every day and watch Monty on his old black and white set, maneuvering the rabbit ears to pick up a clear picture of Monty and the show.

Somehow this got back to Monty.

Monty had never met Bud, or Lou for that matter, but he remembered the old radio show and he remembered their movies.

Monty sent Bud the following letter (and I'm paraphrasing).

> Dear Bud,
>
> I heard through the grapevine that you liked our show and I just wanted you to know how grateful I am. I understand you watch us every day on your black and white set. I'd like you to have a better television picture, so on behalf of all the people who have loved and watched you over the many years, we are sending you a new, big, color television set.

Bud was thrilled to get the letter from Monty, and double-thrilled to receive the color TV.

Four weeks after the television set arrived, Bud Abbott passed away.

*And, so not to leave Jack's stories on a sad note, here's a couple of quickies that Jack threw in.*

Monty was very quick witted ... People would often come up to him and say, "Hi, Monty ... Do you remember me?" And he would say, "Of course I do." And they would say, "What's my name?" And Monty would reply, "If you don't know your own name, how should I know it?"

And in closing ... On one occasion I was with Monty in Palm Springs when a woman came up to him and said, "I understand they named a street after you."

"Yes, that's right."

"What did they name it?"

To which he replied, "Main Street."

# Why Wayne Brady?

MONTY WAS GETTING TIRED. Tired of the grind. Tired of the show.

There were other things he wanted to try. Maybe doing a play, a musical. Or a Las Vegas act. But doing it right this time.

He had done *Let's Make a Deal* from 1968 to 1991. Twenty-seven years. Over 4,500 shows.

It was enough.

But not for the audience.

The show had been off for a while, but in 2009 was coming back. And, of course, everyone thought Monty would be the emcee.

CBS thought Monty would be the emcee.

But Monty told the network it was time for a new face. A younger face.

They auditioned 70 people. Other game show hosts. Comedians. Actors. They auditioned Canadians, Brits, Aussies.

CBS was not happy with any of them.

One night Monty's daughter, Sharon, said, "Did you ever watch Wayne Brady work?"

"Nope."

"You ought to watch *Whose Line Is It Anyway*. They do improv skits. Very funny."

So Monty watched Wayne Brady. He liked what he saw.

So he called him. "Let's have lunch."

Wayne was working in Las Vegas at the time but flew in to have lunch with Monty and some of the CBS people.

Here's how the lunch/interview went.

Monty asked Wayne, "Have you ever seen *Let's Make a Deal*?"

Wayne smiled. "I loved the show."

"Would you like to do the show?"

"Yes."

"Do you THINK you can do the show?"

"Yes, I think I can do it."

"This show's different. You're not standing behind a podium reading questions. It's not that kind of show. In this show you're right in it with the contestants. And they're nervous. And they're excited. For those few minutes together you're in a relationship with them. You gotta show them love! Can you do it?"

"I think so."

"And one more thing," Monty interjected, "don't be an emcee. Be a host."

They made an audition tape with Wayne playing the game. Monty thought he was great. Wayne got the job, and as of this writing he's still going strong. And Monty kept his hand in the show, being credited as a consultant. CBS could not have been more pleased.

The show continues to this date. The ratings are up. It's still a two to three year wait to get tickets. Costumes are more and more outlandish or clever.

And in April of 2018 Wayne won the Daytime Emmy Award for Outstanding Game Show Host for *Let's Make a Deal.*

And all because Sharon asked Monty, "Daddy? Did you ever watch Wayne Brady?"

From left to right, standing, is Mikka Tokuda-Hall (grandchild), Monty, Marilyn, Aaron Gleason (grandchild), Joanna Gleason, Chris Sarandon, Richard Hall. Squatting, left to right, is Maggie Tokuda-Hall (grandchild), Sharon Hall-Kessler, Jack Kessler (grandchild), Todd Kessler, Levy Hall-Kessler.

# Playing *Your First Impression*

## Richard Hall

Richard, Monty's son, has produced several reality shows such as CBS's *Amazing Race*, for which he won an Emmy in 2005. Richard was writer, director, producer for the Emmy-nominated documentary *Death of a Shaman*.

I hadn't written those "questions" for *Your First Impression* in over 50 years, but I thought it might be fun to play the game with Monty's three children. We met with Richard first.

Of course, he did not remember the show, but he turned out to be a damn good "contestant." He gave some great insightful responses, allowing us to get to know his dad on a more personal level.

I would start a sentence and Richard would finish it with the first thing that came to his mind.

Here's how it went, verbatim:

**If my dad could have had dinner with anyone in the world, it would be…** He just about had dinner with everyone in the world. Having said that, he enjoyed having dinner, especially with people like Moshe Dayan*. To that end I think he would have liked to have had dinner with Golda Meir. Funny thing about that is Golda Meir slept in his bed when he was a kid. When she came to visit Winnipeg

* Moshe Dayan - Israeli military head and statesman

his mother, my grandmother, kicked the kids out of their bedroom and the kids had to sleep on the couch so that Golda Meir would have a place to sleep when she visited Winnipeg. Golda Meir was head of Hadassah (the Woman's Zionist Organization of America) out of Milwaukee before she became prime minister of Israel.

I think he would have loved to remind her the time she slept in his bed!

He would also have liked to have dinner with any of his ancestors that he never got a chance to meet from the old country and hear their stories.

**One thing most people didn't know about my dad was…** That he made a mean "matzo brei." He didn't know where the kitchen was except on that rare occasion when he would barricade himself in the kitchen and make "matzo brei."*

**My mom and dad were very different when it came to…** When it came to travel. She wanted to be more adventurous, he wanted to do the classics. He wanted to go see the Mona Lisa while she wanted to go see Mt. Fuji. She would be willing to be uncomfortable if it brought her to a view, while my dad would rather go somewhere to be comfortable and relaxed.

**If I learned anything from my dad it was…** Pay attention to the details.

**If my dad didn't go into show business he would have been a great…** Well, he wanted to be a doctor. But, as you know, they wouldn't let him in to medical school because of the quota. But, he was a people person and a kibitzer so, beside the fact that it's every Jewish mother's dream that her son be a doctor, I think he would've

* Matzo brei - scrambled eggs fried with pieces of Matzo. Served with apple sauce or sour cream or strawberry jam.

been happy running a restaurant. I would say a bar but he didn't drink. He would have loved something where he was interacting with people, hosting and being charming. He would be happy.

**From my mom I learned...** A sense of adventure.

**If you wanted to drive my dad crazy, just...** Leave the lights on! And also, order way too much food for your guests for brunch. If anything was left over he'd say, "Wow! You ordered so much food. Why?!"

**As my dad grew older he began to more and more...** Remember details from his childhood that we had never heard before. We'd hear a story and my sisters and I would look at each other with "What!? Have you ever heard that story before? No, have you? No, I haven't heard it." And that was a up until age 95.

**I'm just like my dad when it comes to...** Rooting for Jewish athletes. We followed our team. He was a diehard Dodgers fan. And, if there was a Jewish player who was also a Dodger that was a perfect storm, of course. But he also cared about Jewish players on other teams, too. Gabe Kaplar was one. Al Rosen was a man he admired a lot.

**I think if my dad had been an animal he would have been...** That's a good one. I think he would have been an exotic talking bird, like a parrot or a macaw. He liked to talk.

**He was at his silliest when...** Doing songs from musicals. He liked to play the piano, though he didn't play that well. He liked to sit next to someone who did play, and he loved to sing songs, especially from the musicals. Sunday mornings he would listen to his LPs, either Itzak Pearlman playing violin or it would be Broadway tunes.

**Talk about politics with my dad and he'd...** He will stand up for people, for people's rights. One hundred percent.

**My dad would never...** Vote Republican.

**My dad's biggest regret probably was...** Not buying the house he rented in Malibu one summer. Years later, he goes, "Do you know what homes in Malibu are worth now?! Oh my god, that little place that we rented..." He would have liked to have been a better real estate baron than he was. He had opportunities that he passed on, but that's like me saying I wish I had bought stock in Apple in 1990.

**Leave my dad alone for a few hours and he'd probably...** Finish the entire *New York Times* crossword puzzles for the entire week.

**One thing he taught me that I'll never forget is...** Well, take care of your kids. Take care of your family.

**His idea of a perfect vacation was...** Sitting out on the beach. Suntan lotion on his white nose. A straw hat on, reading a page-tuner.

Richard called the next day after our interview. "Thinking about what animal he would have been, I think I have a better answer. I think he would have been an elephant. Elephants are very family orientated and they never forget. My dad had an extraordinary memory."

I emailed him back. "It has been so noted. An elephant it is."

## Sharon Hall

Sharon, Monty's youngest, at this writing, is a producer for Sony Pictures Television. She was former president of Endemol Shine Studios. She earned an Emmy nomination for HBO's *Sinatra: All or Nothing at All*. In the past she oversaw development of such series as *Breaking Bad*, *Masters of Sex*, *Damages*, *Justified*, and *Unforgettable*.

We asked Sharon to play *Your First Impression* with us. Here are her answers.

**If my dad could have had dinner with anyone in the world, it would be...** My mom, Marilyn. Endlessly in love with her.

**One thing most people didn't know about my dad was...** He could finish the *New York Times* crossword puzzle in 20 minutes in ink!

**My mom and dad were very different when it came to...** Travel. She sought adventure, he loved relaxation.

**If I learned anything from my dad it was...** Ask questions of others. He loved learning about people.

**If my dad didn't go into show business he would have been a great...** Doctor. He started that way. He had tremendous empathy for others.

**If you wanted to drive my dad crazy, just...** Roll your eyes at him—unacceptable!

**As my dad grew older he began to more and more...** Remember the unvarnished truth about how difficult his young life was.

**I'm just like my dad when it comes to...** Boring people with stories of my kids.

**I think if my dad had been an animal he would have been...** Camel—it was hard to get him to hydrate!

**He was at his silliest when...** There was a baby in the room.

**Talk about politics with my dad and he'd...** Always show his bleeding heart.

**My dad would never...** Pay for valet parking.

**My dad's biggest regret probably was...** That he didn't travel more.

**My dad never stopped believing in...** Us. The most supportive dad in the world.

**Leave my dad alone for a few hours and he'd probably...** Nap.

**One thing he taught me that I'll never forget is...** Marriage is never 50/50. Allow your mate to morph, change is good.

**His idea of a perfect vacation was...** A beach, a novel by Pat Conroy, and my mom!

## Joanne Gleason

In keeping with the Hall tradition of collecting trophies, oldest child actress Joanna has had her share of hardware, too.

She won the Theater World Award in 1977 for her Broadway debut in the musical *I Love My Wife*. She has gone on to have a huge career in Hollywood as well as on Broadway. She won the Drama Desk Award in 1985 for two shows, *It's Only a Place* and *Social Security*, and then hit the jackpot in 1987 with the musical *Into the Woods*, wining the Tony, Outer Critics Circle, and Drama Desk Awards.

Here are her responses about her dad when she played *Your First Impression*.

**If my dad could have had dinner with anyone in the world, it would be...** His mother, Rose. To bring her up to date on family!

**One thing most people didn't know about my dad was...** He could shell pistachios in his mouth.

**My mom and dad were very different when it came to...** Money.

**If I learned anything from my dad it was...** Do for others.

**If my dad didn't go into show business he would have been a great...** Pediatrician.

**If you wanted to drive my dad crazy, just...** Leave the lights on in empty rooms.

**As my dad grew older he began to more and more...** Recall his youth.

**I'm just like my dad when it comes to…** The acrostic in the *New York Times*.

**I think if my dad had been an animal he would have been…** A tortoise. Slow and steady wins the race.

**He was at his silliest when…** The grandkids were around.

**Talk about politics with my dad and he'd…** Get furious about wealthy voting only for their money interests.

**My dad would never…** Give up!

Interesting how different most of their answers were from each other, and yet the sense of love for their parents runs through their answers. We will not analyze their first impressions but leave that possibility to you, the reader. I thought it was great that all three collaborated

Monty's parents, Maurice and Rose Halparin (Year Unknown).

# In Monty's Own Words

*In 2007 Monty sat down with his son, Richard, to record the history of the family for all posterity. Here are excerpts of those tapes in Monty's own words (with a little editing).*

We started this story sixteen years ago when Richard was shooting in New York City and I was in New York on business and Richard said, "How'd you like to come to my studio and talk about the family and get the family's history down on film?"

So we started it. It was 1991. We said we'd continue it at a later date.

It is now 2007. I'm not in New York, but sitting in my home in Beverly Hills. It only took us sixteen years to continue.

## DAD

I was eight or nine when I worked in the butcher shop with my dad and made deliveries first with my sled, later on my bicycle.

But when I turned thirteen my father taught me how to drive a car. I was thirteen, I was this big! But we had to have the car because there were too many deliveries for the bicycle.

I'm thirteen years and ten months old when he takes me out for my first driving lesson. In those days you had to use the clutch. It wasn't automatic, so you had to use the clutch to change gears, and every time I'd switch gears the car would jump up and down.

He took me for that one lesson, we came back to the butcher shop, and he gave me an order to immediately deliver.

My mother said, "But he hasn't learned to drive yet. He's only had one lesson."

My father said, "By the time he gets home he'll know how to drive!"

I took that car and I drove like a bucking bronco! That car was bouncing, jumping, popping the clutch, squealing. But by the time I got home after making the delivery, I knew how to drive!

Another story about my dad that I still remember was when I was still making deliveries on my bicycle.

It was a long night. I started about seven or eight on a Saturday night, and it's twenty or thirty below zero, and I finish the route around eleven. I went into Harmon's drugstore on Portage Avenue to warm up. When I get in there, Mr. Harmon, the pharmacist, looked at me and said, "Young man, what's your name?"

"Monty Halperin," I tell him.

"What are you doing out this late?"

"I'm delivering from my father's butcher shop."

"What's the phone number?"

I told him and he called the store.

"Mr. Halperin? I'm Mr. Harmon from Harmon's Drugstore on Portage Avenue."

"Yes?"

"I've got your son here and he's frozen half to death! What should I do with him?"

My father said, "Thaw him out and put him back on the bicycle."

That was my dad!

My father worked very hard and long hours trying to make

a living. But he was never happy. Never enjoyed working at the butcher shop. He was a strong father. He loved his sons. But he was a rough boss. He was always yelling.

"You're not working fast enough. You're not cleaning up fast enough. You're not washing the dishes fast enough." Everything was "not enough."

Yet, I always respected my father. No matter how hard he made me work in the store, he worked harder.

But it was always a struggle.

When he was younger he drifted from job to job, hardly earning enough money for food and shelter. And the worst part was, whatever little money he made he would take to the local social club and gamble it away playing poker. The more he lost the more he thought his luck would turn any minute.

It never did.

So he'd take out his frustrations at the butcher shop, on my mom, on me, even on the customers. Not a happy man.

Years later, after Monty was a huge success, Monty took his dad out of the butcher shop and bought him a drive-in restaurant in Toronto. The ol' man was as happy as he could be.

"Monty, you don't know what it means to finally take off that butcher's apron."

Now he could wear a suit and carry a briefcase. He could be a businessman, a gentleman.

It was at this time someone offered Monty's father the first Kentucky Fried Chicken franchise for all of Canada. When they began negotiating Monty's father thought the price was too high and turned down the opportunity to own KFC in Canada.

In Monty's words, "Another time in Maurice Halperin's life he made the wrong decision!"

Now, at the drive-in restaurant Monty's father was selling hamburgers for thirty-nine cents. A couple doors over, McDonald's opened and was selling their hamburgers for nineteen cents! Well, all his business left him immediately.

So when the business went bad Monty told him to get rid of it.

So they sold the restaurant. Another loser.

Monty moved his parents to California and bought them a house in Palm Springs.

At the airport in Los Angeles, Monty met his mom and dad with a brand new, luxurious Cadillac.

As they got in the car Monty handed the keys to his father. "Here, you drive."

"I've never driven a Cadillac before. I don't know if I—"

"Just drive it."

So Monty's father drove the car to Monty's house in Beverly Hills.

"What a beautiful car, Monty. I loved driving it."

He started to hand Monty the keys but Monty stopped him.

"Keep the keys, Dad, the car is yours. I bought the car for you."

Monty's father stammered, "I can't drive a Cadillac."

Monty later said, "You have to understand his life. What he went through all his life. The butcher shop, the sickness, the gambling, the drive-in restaurant. Suddenly he's in California and he owns a Cadillac. It was overwhelming."

And they hadn't yet seen the house Monty bought them in Palm Springs.

They called Monty from the Palm Springs house the next day.

"Monty, we are in the Garden of Eden. This house is beautiful. We never lived in a place like this. Outside there's a grapefruit tree, a lemon tree. I can't get over it!"

"Take their happiness and multiply it by a thousand to understand my happiness. And how they appreciated it."

## MOM

My mother was a remarkable woman.

It was my brother, in his speech to Hadassah* where they were honoring our mother, said, "My mother was a doctor who never studied medicine, a lawyer who never passed the bar, she was a nurse, she was a confidant, she was a labor negotiator, she was all these things wrapped up in one human being."

She was also a marriage counselor without certificate, helping couples whose relationships were in trouble.

She raised two boys and still had time to preside over organizations, act and sing in stage plays, and head fundraising drives to help those in need. She had a magnetic personality, said those who knew her. Spoke often at charity events, and above anyone, had the greatest influence on my life.

I wanted to follow in her footsteps, be a singer, actor, storyteller like my mom.

She wanted me to be a doctor.

When I couldn't get into medical school she may have been disappointed, but she soon beamed with his success. Showing pride, however, was not part of the family DNA. For instance, after em-

* Hadassah - The Women's Zionist Organization of America

ceeing my first game show I said to my mom, "Well, Mother, what do you think of your star now?"

To which she responded, "When you replace Ed Sullivan, *then* you'll be a star."

A year after they moved to Palm Springs Monty's mother went back to Toronto because cancer was spreading rapidly through her body and her days were numbered.

Before they could leave the Springs, as weak as his mother was and as bad as she felt, she wanted to fulfill her commitment to speak at the Palm Springs Hadassah Club.

So Monty's father took her. In her life she probably spoke at over one-hundred Hadassah meetings. She spoke brilliantly. No one suspected this woman was suffering. She got back in the car and said, "I have nothing left, I am so tired."

## BOB

Let me tell you about my brother, Bob. He followed in my footsteps. We're six years apart but extremely close. We talked all the time.

He followed me to Toronto. We got him a job at a radio station, but he didn't last long. He decided he really wanted to go to law school. He got married. His wife went to work, I helped them, and he became a lawyer.

Bob had two kids. Both are lawyers, too. His daughter, Barbara, lived in Italy, spoke eight languages, and was a translator for the United Nations. Loved Rome. She had offers to move elsewhere, Vienna, wouldn't leave Rome. She was brilliant and beautiful.

Bob also had a son, Andy, the youngest. He was everybody's favorite. Great personality. All the nieces were crazy about him.

Bob and his family were all talented and all well-respected.

Here's something. Six years after I was elected president of the International Variety Club, Bob was elected president of the club.

I called my father in Palm Springs. I said, "Dad, a *second* son of yours is now the president of the International Variety Club."

And he said, "Well, they finally got the right one!"

After that, Bob became the house attorney for the club. He did that job for over twenty-five years. Never charged the club a penny. All pro bono. Not for a secretary, not for a stamp, not for a phone call.

That's my brother Bob.

The most important part of my life has been my charity work. Inherited from my grandfather, my mother, and down to me, and hopefully to my children and my grandchildren.

In my house you can see hundreds of awards that I've received, others in the garage and so on. That's for my life's work. Honors from the Order of Canada to the International Humanitarian Award from the International Variety Club and so on and so on.

It's what I want to leave to my children and my grandchildren.

Not long ago I received an award from the lawyers of Los Angeles. These are the pro bono lawyers, the ones who work for charities. There were 1,500 people at the Century Plaza Hotel. They gave the William O. Douglas Awards named for Judge Douglas and called the Justice Awards. I received the award for Justice in Entertainment.

And in my speech I said, "They say I've raised around one billion dollars for charity. I said I don't like the expression 'giving back'. You know the line, 'He's giving back to the community.' It sounds like I took something out and then gave it back. It's an expression that means well but is not the right thing."

In my family, in my life, doing work for others in charity or philanthropy, helping others, it's an obligation, it's a duty, it's a responsibility. In our family it's the Eleventh Commandment. *Thou shall do because it must be done, it should be done, and you do it.*

And I've always believed in that. You do it because it should be done.

## JOANNA

My family? As I've said many times, I'm proud of my family.

Joanna? From the time she was a baby I knew she was destined for the stage. When she was in her crib she used to do summersaults to get attention!

And yet, when she had her second or third birthday we came with a camera to film it and she cried for us to turn the camera off because she was frightened of it. And now, look at all the TV shows she has done in front of the camera!

Joanna grew up to be a great actress. Smart girl who still does the *New York Times* crossword puzzle in ink. She went to Broadway and has starred in ten Broadway shows.

She won the Tony Award for the Best Actress in the musical *Into the Woods*.

And she got the Dramatist Award and the Newcomer Award and has been nominated for many others. Great singer, dancer, comedienne, actress. A very talented, beautiful lady.

We call her the "diva" in our family.

That's my Joanna.*

---

* Joanna has since been nominated for the Tony, Outer Critics Circle, and Drama Desk awards for the musical *Dirty Rotten Scoundrels*. She has appeared in dozens of TV shows and numerous movies.

## RICHARD

Richard is as solid as the Rock of Gibraltar. When Richard was in public school he was elected president of his class, president of the school. When he went to high school he ran for president of the high school. He and his friends thought Richard was such a shoo-in, they didn't vote. Richard lost by two votes. He learned in politics to leave no stone unturned!

Then he went to Yale and edited either the school magazine or newspaper. He was always a rebel and would personally invite many subversives to speak on campus.

After graduating from Yale he eventually moved back to California and turned his attention to television and film production. He won the Emmy for producing CBS' *The Amazing Race* series and has produced numerous reality shows, documentaries, and feature films.

## SHARON

Last but not least, is my baby, Sharon. Sharon came along twelve years after Richard was born, a big surprise to our family, and what a delightful addition she has been. She is something else.

Sharon, who had graduated Tufts University, attended a reunion and met a man who had gone to Tufts a few years before her.

I love the way he proposed to her. She was in a studio testing some people for some show she was producing and he came on the set while she's auditioning actors, giving them screen tests, and he proposed to her.

Naturally, she accepted, especially after she saw the "screen test" of him proposing! It seems the whole crew was in on the proposal except Sharon.

Sharon has gone on to be a successful television producer.

Ingrid Bergman and Marilyn during the making of *Golda Meir* (1982).]

# Marilyn and Ingrid

LET ME TELL YOU what kind of a woman Marilyn is. She was an actress who gave up her acting, and when we came out to California she wrote book reviews for *The LA Times* and sold a couple of television shows, one, *Love, American Style*, starring myself.

Here's an interesting story about Marilyn. She read in the newspaper that Paramount Pictures was considering doing a movie based on the life of Golda Meir. So she called Paramount and spoke to the producer, Harve Bennett.

Bennett told his secretary that he'd meet with Marilyn as a courtesy to Monty Hall, who did so much good charity work.

Marilyn went into Paramount, met Bennett, and had this conversation:

"Mr. Bennett, what do you know about Israel?"

"Not much." Bennett shrugged. "Why?"

"That's why I'm here. What do you know about Golda Meir?"

Bennett shrugged again.

Marilyn continued. "Well, I know a lot about Golda Meir, and I don't think you can make this movie without me. You're going to need my advice."

They spent an hour together, after which he hired her to work on the picture.

"I don't know what you're going to do," says Bennett, "as associate producer or consultant. I just know I've got to have you on this picture!"

And off she went to Israel.

The question then came up, "Who's going to play the part of Golda?"

Paramount tried to get Ingrid Bergman, but she turned them down. So while they're looking for another actress, Marilyn and I went to a Variety International Convention in London. Ingrid Bergman was invited, and she sat at the head table next to us!

I lean over to Marilyn and say, "Marilyn, change places with me and go to work."

So Marilyn sat next to Bergman and told her she must make this movie. She must play Golda Meir.

Ingrid smiled and said, "Listen, Mrs. Hall, Marilyn, how can I, a tall, Nordic, gentile woman be a short, clumpy Jewish lady?"

Marilyn said, "You weren't Catholic but you played Joan of Arc."

Ingrid Bergman broke out laughing. She could hardly catch her breath. Finally she said, "Do you have a script with you? Will you meet me in my flat tomorrow afternoon?"

So the next afternoon they met. And Bergman loved the script. And she loved Marilyn. But she worried, "How can I play her right? Listen, I won't play her unless I can take a screen test."

Marilyn said, "You don't have to take a screen test. They're *waiting* for you at Paramount."

"No, I have to convince myself."

So arrangements were made. A wig, make-up, padding. And they did the test.

When it was done Bergman looked at the film they shot and everyone held their breath.

She pointed at the image on the screen and said, "That's not Ingrid up there. That's Golda. Alright, I'll do it."

And that's how they got Ingrid Bergman to do the movie.

So Marilyn went back to Israel. She was supposed to only be there three weeks, but then she called me. "We're going to be an extra three weeks."

At the end of the ninth week I'm on a plane to Israel to see what my wife looks like!

And she was busy. She was on the phone talking to newspapers around the world who all wanted to know the latest about Ingrid Bergman. She was busy on the sets, busy on locations, busy with the shooting.

And she never left Ingrid's side. The two went everywhere together. So I got a driver and played tourist, revisiting many places I had been to earlier times.

On the last day of shooting in Israel the local movie theater played *For Whom the Bell Tolls*. Ingrid was nineteen when she made that film.

In the theater she sat with Marilyn and me, and about fifteen minutes into the movie she whispered to us, "It's too hard to see myself at nineteen." And with that she got up and left.

As they were breaking down the set the next day she came over to me and said, "Thank you for giving us your wife," and she gave me a big hug and a kiss.

We never saw her again. But she and Marilyn would continue to talk on the phone when we came back to Beverly Hills.

On that last day of shooting Ingrid kept muffing her lines. The director chided her gently, "The great Ingrid Bergman muffing her lines?!"

And she answered, "I just didn't want it to end."

I always wondered, did she mean the movie or her life? I always wondered if she knew she was dying of cancer and that four months later she would be dead.

When Ingrid was told she was nominated for an Emmy for her portrayal of Golda Meir, she called Marilyn and said, "I'm too sick to attend, but if I win I want you to accept the award for me."

What a wonderful thing to say to just an associate producer who she befriended on the film.

Marilyn was overcome. But when Paramount heard that a lowly associate producer was going to accept the award for Bergman they told her no, that the head of the studio or the producer of the film would accept.

Marilyn was furious. After all, this was Ingrid Bergman's wish, not the studio's.

So Marilyn got on the phone and called Pia Lindstrom, Ingrid's daughter who lived in New York.

"Please, Pia, come out to LA and accept the Emmy for your mother if she wins. I don't want those bastards from the studio to take it."

Pia came. Ingrid won for Best Actress. Pia accepted the award on behalf of her mother.

Marilyn went on to associate produce and then produce other films. She also remained most active supporting the Julie Ann Singer Child Care Center, Guardians of Courage, Wallis Annenberg Center for the Performing Arts, the Jewish Welfare Fund, the Jewish Home for the Aged, Brandeis University, and Tel Aviv University, while serving on the board of trustees of Variety Clubs International.

And somewhere found the time to publish two cookbooks!

Not bad for a woman who, at that time, was 81 years old.

# The Humanitarian

Away from *Let's Make a Deal*, Monty worked tirelessly for a variety of charities. Through his efforts, his personal appearances, and his fund raising, Monty helped raise an estimated one billion dollars! That's with a B.

He received over 500 honorary awards and served as president and later chairman of the board of Variety Clubs International, the world's largest children's charity.

There are four children's hospital wings named after Monty: UCLA Medical Center, Hahnemann Hospital in Philadelphia, Mt. Sinai in Toronto, and Johns Hopkins in Baltimore.

His contribution to the television arts have honored him with three Walk of Fames: Hollywood, Palm Springs, and Toronto.

He served as Hollywood's honorary mayor from 1973 to 1979. In 2013 Monty received television's Lifetime Achievement Award.

He was the recipient of Canada's two most prestigious awards: The Order of Canada, a national honor, and from his home province, the Order of Manitoba.

How many speeches did Monty make in a lifetime? Dozens and dozens.

And he would start each one with a different story. He loved telling stories, some factual, some just jokes.

Here are some of his favorites.

He told this story when he spoke at a Jewish home luncheon.

"Two Jewish families lived in a small town outside of Winnipeg. In the whole town there were only these two Jewish families, the Friedmans and the Coopersteins, who were neighbors.

"One day, the Friedman's young son is coming home from school when two tough non-Jewish bullies grab him to beat him up.

"'Why do you wanna beat me up?' asked the boy.

'Because you killed our Lord. You killed Jesus!'

"'No,' said the boy. 'It wasn't us. It was the Coopersteins next door!'"

Monty committed to go to Vancouver to speak at a Hadassah bazaar. Hadassah is a woman's Jewish club that actively supports Israel. They wanted to pay him a fee but Monty objected, saying he never took fees when he appeared at a fundraiser. And especially this one, since his mother was national vice president of Canada's Hadassah.

Instead, what Monty asked for was an airplane ticket for he and Marilyn and a hotel room.

The lady from Hadassah called Monty back and said, "We'll pay the airfare, but not for the hotel."

I called my mother in Toronto and told her the story.

"Ma, I waived the $5,000 appearance fee but they won't pay the $70 a night for the hotel! I hate to go over that lady's head, but you're vice president!"

To which his mother responded, "Good for them. You can afford it better than they can!"

"Go fight with a Hadassah Mother!"

Another time, years later, when his mother was close to death, Monty flew up to Toronto to visit her in the hospital. "I told her I was doing my first television special for ABC at the same time I was asked to be the keynote speaker at yet another Hadassah National Convention.

"My mother was thrilled. She was lying in bed and she whispered to me, 'Make it the best you ever did.'

"I asked, 'The ABC Special?'

"She said, 'No. The Hadassah speech.'"

For 31 years Monty gave a little speech at the opening of the Monty Hall Tennis Tournament, raising money for the Cedars-Sinai Hospital in Beverly Hills on behalf of diabetes.

One year he started with this story.

"I know it wasn't easy to find a parking space this morning. It reminded me of this man who was looking for a parking space on the street in Beverly Hills. He was late for a meeting. He drove around and around. Nothing.

"So he prayed to God. He said, 'God, if you find me a parking space I'll promise to go to church every Sunday. I'll be better to my employees. I'll spend more quality time with my wife and kids. If only you find me a parking space.'

"Suddenly a huge Lincoln left a spot right in front of the man, for which he said, 'Never mind, God, I found one!'"

Speaking at a Vancouver senior residence charity event, Monty opened with this story.

"Two older husbands are in the living room while their two wives are in the kitchen.

"One husband asks the other, 'Seen any good movies lately?'

"'The other one responded, 'Oh, we saw a terrific one.'

"'What was the name of it?'

"'It was…' He couldn't remember. He was having a *senior moment.*

"'I should remember. We saw it only on Tuesday.'

"He turned to his friend. 'What do you call a red flower that has thorns on its stem?'

"The other husband answered, 'A rose?'

"The first husband got excited. 'That's it!' Then calling into the kitchen, "Rose, what was the name of the movie...'

The seniors in the home loved that story.

One last one. Monty was speaking at a fundraiser for either the ASPCA, or the Humane Society.

"Benny Mandel bought a donkey from an old farmer for $100. The farmer promised to deliver the donkey the next day.

"When the farmer drove up he said he had some bad news. The donkey had died.

"'Well, then give me my money back,' said Benny.

"'Can't do that. I went and spent it already.'

"'Okay,' said Benny. 'Just unload the donkey.'

"'But he's dead.'

"'I won't tell anybody.'

"A month later, the farmer ran into Benny.

"'What did you do with that dead donkey?'

"'I raffled him off. I sold 500 tickets at five dollars a piece and made a profit of $2,500!'

"'Didn't anyone complain?' asked the farmer.

"'Just the guy who won. So I gave him his five dollars back!'"

Yes, Monty loved to tell a good joke. And he always tried to tell a story appropriate for the organization he was speaking to.

He once said, "When I speak to an audience, my success is measured in applause and laughter. And don't kid yourself, applause and laughter still mean more to a performer than money!"

But joking aside, Monty's appearances to raise precious dollars for children to senior citizens has saved and extended the life of only God knows how many.

Whether monies were needed for research or building a wing

or money for a parish to stay afloat, Monty always seemed to make himself available.

Monty never forgot the near-poverty he grew up with. He was also quite sickly as a child, almost dying of pneumonia. It was easy for Monty to identify with the "have-nots" and the people who suffered.

And he never forgot his mother, who was Monty's muse, his source of inspiration. His mom was a singer and actress, but also a great speaker who worked for numerous charitable organizations. As Monty grew up he followed in her footsteps.

When Monty moved to Toronto he became president of the Variety Club of Canada. They would hold telethons to raise funds for disadvantaged children. Now there are chapters in eleven countries paying for artificial limbs and care for burn victims and guidance for physically and mentally abused children, along with other maladies.

But before there were telethons it wasn't easy to raise money.

On Sunday afternoons, when baseball stadiums and movie theaters were closed because of Toronto's Blue Laws, Monty and Marilyn would take cans of a feature film with a tap dancer and an accordion player and go off to some town outside Ottawa where they'd open up the theater and admission was free.

People would fill the theater. Then Monty would play the first half of the movie, turn off the projector, bring out the tap dancer and the accordion player, and Monty would sing a couple of songs before making the pitch for the Variety Club. Monty and Marilyn would pass tin cans around the theater and raise all kinds of money. Then they'd play the second half of the movie.

They'd then pile everyone in the car with the cans of film and drive two and a half hours back to Toronto, not getting home till the wee hours.

But they did it every weekend. As exhausted as they might have been, both Monty and Marilyn knew they were helping to build a wing or a hospital for children.

Monty continued to work for the Variety Club in New York. But when he came to California in 1961 and had his success on television, he became more and more sought after.

Monty always made himself available if it were for a worthy cause.

Monty would emcee, do the auctions, and make speeches. He never charged a penny for his appearances. The more he did, the more he was sought after. He would do over sixty appearances a year.

By the time he retired he had emceed well over 100 telethons for the Variety Club and, with the hundreds of appearances for other charities, I repeat, he helped raise an estimated one billion dollars.

He will be missed. He and Marilyn will be missed.

Marilyn Hall 1927 - 2017
Monty Hall 1921 - 2017
Together Seventy Years...
and counting

# CREDITS*

## Television Appearances

### Series

Host, *The Little Revue,* 1953

Host, *Floor Show,* 1953

Host, *Matinee Party,* 1953

Anchor, *Monitor,* NBC, 1955-1960

Host and narrator, Cowboy Theatre, NBC, 1956-1957

Emcee, Keep Talking, CBS, 1958-1959, then ABC, 1959-1960

Host, *Byline: Monty Hall,* CBS, 1959

Emcee, *Video Village,* CBS, 1960

Emcee, *Let's Make a Deal,* NBC, 1963-1968, ABC, 1968-1977, revived from Vancouver, British Columbia, and syndicated, 1980

Host, *NBC Comedy Playhouse* (also known as *Bob Hope Presents the Chrysler Theatre, The Chrysler Theater,* and *Universal Star Time*), NBC, 1968

Host, *It's Anybody's Guess,* NBC, 1977

Host, *Beat the Clock* (also known as *The All-New Beat the Clock*), CBS, 1979-1980

Host, *The All-New Let's Make A Deal* (also known as *Let's Make A Deal*), CBS, 1984-1986

---

* http://www.filmreference.com/film/57/Monty-Hall.html#ixzz5J6auUjTh

Host, *Split Second,* syndicated, 1986-1987

Host, *Let's Make a Deal,* NBC, 1990-1991

Made television debut as substitute emcee, *Strike It Rich,* CBS; also appeared on *Fun in the Morning.*

## Pilots

Host, *Madhouse 90,*ABC, 1972

General Sam Brewster, *The Courage and the Passion,* NBC, 1978

## Specials

*Li'l Abner,* NBC, 1971

Himself, *ABC Funshine Saturday Sneak Peek,*1974

*Mitzi and a Hundred Guys,* CBS, 1975

Host, *Lights, Camera, Monty!,* ABC, 1975

Host, *Monty Hall's Variety Hour,* ABC, 1976

*Those Wonderful TV Game Shows,* NBC, 1984

*All-Star Party for Lucille Ball,* CBS, 1984

*An All-Star Party for "Dutch" Reagan,* CBS, 1985

*All Star Party for Clint Eastwood,* CBS, 1986

Host, *Split Second*, syndicated, 1987

Guest, *It's Howdy Doody Time*(also known as *It's Howdy Doody Time: A 40-Year Celebration*), syndicated, 1987

Host, *All-Star Party for Joan Collins,*CBS, 1987

*The Television Academy Hall of Fame,* Fox, 1990

Host, *The Comedy Concert II,*TNN, 1990

Himself, *Bob Crane: The E! True Hollywood Story,*E! Entertainment Television, 1998

## Episodic

Monty Hall, "Let's Make a Deal," *The Odd Couple*, ABC, 1973

"Love and the Man of the Year," *Love, American Style*, ABC, 1973

*Rowan & Martin's Laugh-In,* 1973

Voice of Monty Hall, "Mama Loves Monty," *Wait `till Your Father Gets Home* (animated), syndicated, 1974

Himself, "A Different Drummer," *The Odd Couple*, ABC, 1974

Harry Morrison, "The Parents Know Best/A Selfless Love/Nubile Nurse," *The Love Boat*, ABC, 1978

Guest, *Password Plus,* 1979

Himself, "Calendar Girl," *Jennifer Slept Here,* 1983

"The Test," *The Wonder Years,* ABC, 1992

Himself, "The Taxman Cometh," *The Nanny*, CBS, 1996

Himself, "The Long and Winding Short Cut," *Sabrina, the Teenage Witch,* ABC, 1999

Himself, "Monty Hall: Let's Make a Deal," B*iography, Arts and Entertainment*, 1999

"Parenthood," *Providence*, NBC, 2001

Himself, "The Promise Ring," *That '70s Show*, Fox, 2001

Himself, "Talent Show," *The Surreal Life*, 2003

Himself, "Talent Show," *Let's Make a Deal*, 2003

Himself, "Game Show Week," *The Hollywood Squares*, 2003

Also appeared in *That Girl,* ABC; *The Flip Wilson Show,* NBC; *The Dean Martin Show,* NBC; as himself, *Love & War,* CBS; and as himself, *The Charlie Horse Music Pizza,* PBS.

## Television Work

### Series

Executive producer, *Your First Impression,* NBC, 1960

Creator and producer (with Stefan Hatos), *Let's Make a Deal,* beginning 1963

Executive producer, *Masquerade Party,* syndicated, 1974

Executive producer, *The McLean Stevenson Show,* NBC, 1976

Executive producer, *It's Anybody Guess,* NBC, 1977

Executive producer, *Split Second,* 1986

Creator, *Let's Make a Deal,* 1990

Creator, *Big Deal,* Fox, 1996

Executive producer and creator, *Let's Make a Deal,* 2003

### Film Appearances

*The Canadian Conspiracy,* 1986

(Uncredited) Himself, *Off the Menu: The Last Days of Chasen's,* 1997

### Stage Appearances; Major Tours

Lead role, *High Button Shoes,* U.S. cities, 1978

## WRITINGS

### Television Pilots

*For the People,* 1986

### Books

(With Bill Libby) *Emcee: Monty Hall,* Grosset & Dunlap, 1973

### Newsletters

*Memo from Monty,* 1955

# About Ken Rotcop

KEN ROTCOP WON THE Writers Guild Award, The Neil Simon Award, and the Image Award for writing and producing the television movie *For Us, The Living: The Story of Medgar Evers.*

He was also the recipient of the Unity Award for writing the best television documentary series Images of America for CBS. Ken was the creative head of four studios: Hanna-Barbera, Avco Embassy Pictures, Cannon Films, and TransWorld Productions.

He is the author of the best-selling series of books *The Perfect Pitch: How to Sell Yourself And Your Movie Idea To Hollywood, Remembering Marvin Kaplan*, and *As I Remember It: My 50 Year Career as an Award Winning Writer, Producer, and Studio Executive.* His four DVDs on writing, pitching, and selling your scripts, including *Let's Sell Your Script!*, are in bookstores and colleges everywhere.

Sadly, Ken passed away in late 2018. He leaves behind his wife Connie and his two daughters and grandchildren. Ken also leaves us with an unmatched legacy of writing, movies, and generosity of his time, creative expertise, and heart. No one has done more than Ken for the writers of his workshops and PitchMart, Hollywood, and around the globe. We will all miss him dearly.

For more information about this book, *Remembering Monty Hall*, contact co-author Kimberly Kaplan at www.kimberlykaplan.com.

# About Kimberly Kaplan

AUTHOR AND MOTHER OF an autistic boy, Kim wrote *A Parents' Guide to Early Autism Intervention*, which is a useful guide for parents who are just beginning their autism journey. Another source for autism-related information came from writing her autism-related blog on the website, www.modernmom.com. A compilation was published entitled, *Two Years of Autism Blogs Featured on* ModernMom.com.

Her ebook, *Warsaw Freedom*, is the story of two Jewish women who are smuggled out of the Warsaw Ghetto during World War II.

Her screenplays include *Warsaw*, *Max* and *The Happy Prince*, *Corgi*, *Parent Boot Camp*, and *Scam*. She is a produced screenwriter with credits, *Don't Fall Asleep* (Amazon, iTunes), *Safeword*, and her autism-related film short, *Autism and Cake*, starring Ed Asner, who plays a grandfather who struggles to accept his autistic grandson.

She blogs on the website www.modernmom.com weekly, tweets on @tipsautismmom, and you can find her on LinkedIn.

CPSIA information can be obtained
at www.ICGtesting.com
Printed in the USA
LVHW021601150419
614225LV00014B/326/P

9 781629 334233